Roots to Thrive

An evidence-informed guide to resilience & well-being

By Shannon Dames and the Roots to Thrive Community

Within each of us lives the wisdom to heal and the courage to thrive

ISBN: 978-1-0698885-0-1

Notice
This publication is for educational purposes only and is not a substitute for professional medical or therapeutic advice. The author and publisher assume no responsibility for the use or misuse of the material contained herein.

Cover design by Phillip Dames
Lead Editor: Michelle Brewer
Printed in Canada
First Edition, 2026
Nanaimo, BC

The Roots of Roots

Roots to Thrive began as a seed—a response to the growing mental health crisis among healthcare providers.

In 2018, it started with gatherings in coffee shops and living rooms, inspired by a shared intention. We came not only as clinicians, spiritual care providers, and cultural knowledge holders, but as human beings committed to *walking the path ourselves—and walking it together.* Many of us carried our own lived experience of burnout, united by a desire to find resilient ground and map a way from surviving to thriving.

These early conversations contributed to an initial seedbed that formally emerged through my doctoral research and thesis. That soil has since been enriched and carefully tended by the inspirations of many others—creating the conditions that support the Roots to Thrive framework's ongoing growth, refinement, and capacity to respond within a rapidly changing world.

We integrate Western theory and science, wisdom shared by local Indigenous knowledge holders—with Snuneymuxw Elder Geraldine Manson serving as lead Elder since 2018—and perennial spiritual teachings. Together, these sources converge around *core ingredients that help humans transition from surviving to thriving.*

An earlier version of this work was published as a textbook with Elsevier to address the roots of burnout and the growing rates of mental health conditions among professionals working in trauma-laden environments (Dames, 2022).

This guide explains the roots of the framework—*the why*—and offers practical tips and practices to help the learning shift from knowing what to *do*, to embodying how to *be.*

In 2020, we received grant funding to research the application of our resilience-informed community practice model to psychedelic-assisted therapy. Under the guidance of Dr. Pamela Kryskow, ketamine-assisted therapy was introduced in 2020, followed by psilocybin in 2021 and MDMA in 2024—each offered as an optional pathway for participants with persistent mental health conditions.

Today, RTT continues to grow through cycles of research and feedback from participants and practitioners. And we remain what we've always been: a relational, evolving community of practice—a place where science and spirit meet, and where healing unfolds in relationship. As a familiar saying goes,

"We're all just walking each other home." (Ram Dass & Gorman, 1985)

Acknowledgements

To all the knowledge keepers, clinicians, researchers, staff, volunteers, alumni, students, and community partners—your wisdom, feedback, and care continue to co-create this tapestry, woven from many voices and teachings, each thread helping shape the path ahead.

While this guide began with my doctoral research on resilience, it continues to evolve through the insight of participants, experts, and Elders. It's brought to life by the words, quotes, and poetry shared by team members and participants.

Crosbie Watler, Wes Taylor, Helen Watler, Darlus Jonsson, Todd Haspect, and Julia Sheffield strengthened several supporting sections through their contributions. Pam Kryskow is the primary author for Appendices D and F; Helen Watler and Darlus Jonsson for Appendix G; and Phillip Dames for Appendix H.

Special thanks to Michelle Brewer for her generous and meticulous editing throughout the publication process, and to Susan James for her editing support.

Since 2018, countless individuals have contributed their insight, written and reviewed materials, facilitated cohorts, nurtured learning spaces, and walked beside participants with authenticity and compassion. Many additional hands and hearts have supported the initial innovation and development of this shared path, including:

Alexa Garrey	Deborah Irvine	Jessica Fraser	LoriAnne Demers	Rebecca Sanders
Allan Campbell	Della Rice	Jim Parker	Marcia McMillan	Rob Laurie
Andrea Lemp	Duncan Grady	Jimena Garcia	Margaret Huml	Robyn Bartle
Andrej Klimo	Emily Webster	Jo Hall	Mark Sanders	Roisin Mulligan
Barb Fehlau	Emmy Manson	Jody Millward	Marnie Roper	Ruth Dantzer
Barb Simoes	Eric Eligh	Jolene Bloomfield	Matthew Ta	Ryan Boyer
Bill Simoes	Erika Gagnon	Julia Sheffield	Michelle Brewer	Sarah Corrin
Billy Wilton	Erin Ryding	Julian Noris	Michelle Gagnon	Scott Elliott
Blake Hunter	Gail Peekeekoot	Kaarina Lenk	Mike Bernard	Shelley Genovesse
Brittany Boyer	Gayle McCue	Kate Wilton	Nan Seward	Steve Fraser
Candace Neyck	Geraldine Manson	Kelsey Voyer	Nicole Vaugeois	Susan James
Christine Dennstedt	Graham Blackburn	Kerrie Miller	Nikki Klassen	Tamara Pearl
Cindy Trytten	Graham Walker	Keva Glynn	Pam Kryskow	Todd Haspect
Claerwen Sladen	Griffin Russell	Krys Sciberras	Patricia O'Hagan	Uta Sbotofrankenstein
Clark Lewis	Heather Straight	Kyle Greenway	Paul Stamets	Valorie Masuda
Crosbie Watler	Helen Watler	Lara Jeletzky	Pearl Allard	Vivian Tsang
Crystal Fee	Jacqueline Neligan	Laura Brace	Peg Peters	Wendy Young
Darlus Jonsson	Jade Se	Laura McLean	Peter Roeck	Wes Taylor
Dave Frank	Jeannette Watts	Leah Mallen	Philippe Lucas	Zhiish McKenzie
Deb Charrois	Jenn Wyse	Lindsay Risk	Phillip Dames	

With deep appreciation for the generous support of *Research BC, Island Health Authority, Vancouver Island University*, the *Simoes Family, Hope Initiative Foundation, Kindred Trust, Daffy Foundation, Parker Foundation, MAPS Canada, BC Nurses' Union, BC Fire Fighters Association, Health Connect, Circadian Labs,* collaborating *First Nations*, philanthropic partners, and several government and community supported grants.

We also acknowledge the careful use of AI-assisted tools to help refine language for accessibility and clarity, and to generate images that bring key concepts to life—supporting our intention to make this work as inclusive and comprehensible as possible.

A Note about Formats

This resource is available in multiple formats, including print, eBook, and audiobook, to support different learning preferences and accessibility needs. You can access the various formats through the following link: https://books2read.com/Roots-to-Thrive-Book

A Note about Sharing

As with all shared work, the knowledge shared here arises from many voices, woven together in the spirit of reciprocity. You're welcome to carry forward any teachings that resonate with you, weaving them into your own journey. To support knowledge integrity and honour the people and traditions that inform this work, please seek permission before reproducing or distributing written material.

Preface and Practical Aspects

We live in a time of profound change—social, economic, ecological, and spiritual—where uncertainty often feels like a constant. These shifts can leave us uneasy, searching for steady ground.

We can't offer quick fixes or certainty. What we can do is walk with you and share perspectives and practices that have helped many of us find our footing when the ground feels unstable.

Here, we recognize that resilience isn't about resisting the storm. It's about staying rooted, adapting with grace, accepting what we can't change, and investing our energy where we can. We remember that healing isn't about fixing ourselves; it's about feeling safe and clear enough to release what no longer serves—so we can meet life with open hands.

We offer a meeting place—bringing resilience theory, research, transpersonal psychology, and perennial teachings into relationship. It's shaped by voices from many walks of life: clinicians, Indigenous Knowledge Keepers, and community members whose contributions bring depth, richness, and relatability.

The Waypoints and practices in these pages aren't just for RTT participants—they address universal human needs, rooted in four pillars of resilience: *awareness*, *regulation*, *compassion*, and *alignment*. Their form may differ across cultures, but the underlying principles are universal. And while we have much in common, we are also unique. You are welcome to adapt what you find here in ways that fit your wants, needs, and the context and culture that informs you.

Acknowledging Complexities and Inequities

Healing doesn't happen in isolation. Our wounds aren't just personal—they're generational, carried through our families, communities, and the systems that shape us. Naming this matters because resilience grows not by looking away, but by creating spaces where we make sense—where our experiences are understood in the context of the histories and structures that formed them.

We acknowledge that systemic inequities and racism are woven into society, healthcare, and yes—they also show up in our own practices. We commit to keep learning, listening, and interrupting these patterns—individually and collectively.

A Note About Repetition (By Intention)

You'll revisit certain ideas and practices more than once. This repetition is intentional. Learning—especially nervous-system learning—deepens through returning, re-encountering, and integrating. As you move through the Waypoints, familiar concepts will meet you at new stages of readiness.

From Understanding to Embodying

The mind can recognize a truth, but it's the body and heart that learn to trust it. Transformation happens in that deeper knowing—one we embody through practice, repetition, and relationship. To support this shift, we've woven poetry, reflection prompts, and simple practices throughout this guide.

Embodiment takes time. It often begins with fleeting moments of feeling a bit clearer and steadier. As these moments add up, effort gradually gives way to ease, and we learn to move at what Dr. Pamela Kryskow, an RTT physician and long-time team member, calls *the pace of trust*—honouring our timing, our limits, and the call that fuels our courage.

Many of us have tried to walk this path alone, only to find we couldn't break through. That's not failure—it's part of our learning. Like trees that root together in a forest, we're strongest in our interconnection—steadying one another in storms and sharing nutrients when resources are thin.

Preparation and Reading Approach

If you're reading this, preparation has already begun. The following *optional* practices can help your mind and body get ready for the deeper work ahead:

- **Notice sensations and emotions.** As you move through your day, notice what feelings or sensations show up—or notice if nothing comes up. Nothing to do. Just notice.
- **Reflect on younger selves.** Look at old photographs. Notice changes in your eyes or smile over time. It can help to ask people what they remember about you as a child and what brought you joy.
- **Notice admiration and irritation.** People we admire often reflect qualities waiting to emerge. People who irritate us can point to parts we've hidden to feel safe.

You can explore these practices at your own pace or follow along with the 12-week Roots to Thrive program, where each Waypoint aligns with the week's focus.

Walking It Out

As we move along this path, it's not about becoming something new—it's a return to what's always been there, waiting beneath layers ready to be shed. Life's waves don't stop, but with awareness and resourcing, we learn to ride them. What was once overwhelming becomes something we can meet with confidence. We shift from keeping our heads above water to remembering we're held by the ocean itself—less fixated on the waves, more anchored in what carries us. From this grounded place, guided by an inner compass that already knows the way, we learn to trust life's rhythms—no longer swimming against the currents, but moving with the flow of all that is.

Table of Contents

WAYPOINT 1: FOUNDATIONS & INTENTIONS

This first Waypoint takes us a little deeper into the ideas that shape Roots to Thrive (RTT). For some, theory might not land—or it might even feel irritating. That's okay! For others, understanding the *why* behind what we do can help build trust and confidence in the process.

Think of theory like a map. It doesn't tell us exactly where to step, but it helps us keep our bearings when the path gets unclear. The goal isn't to memorize the map—it's to have something to orient us when we get lost.

You can skim it, skip it, or come back to it later when it feels more relevant. We include perennial teachings and research because a sense of *why* becomes especially important when the road gets bumpy. When fear clouds our vision, it's easy to lose sight of where we're headed. Our *why* becomes the steady point on the horizon—offering the meaning that makes courage possible.

Meaning > Fear = Courage

It's not exactly a scientific formula—but research does back it up. Studies on psychological flexibility show that when people's actions are aligned with their values, purpose, or a sense of belonging, they become more able to face challenges with confidence (Watts & Luoma, 2020; Sloshower et al., 2024). This alignment inspires us to act—not from fear, but from meaning.

Courage isn't willpower or fearlessness. If we could've willed our way out of suffering, we would've done it by now. Courage becomes possible when something matters enough that the risk is worth taking—with fear still present, we move forward anyway (Pury et al., 2024; Chowkase et al., 2024).

Starting Whole

We don't see you as broken. You've always carried what you need—it's often just been buried under layers of survival. Healing is remembering what's been yours all along.

Wholeness isn't about having it all together. It's about sitting with the mess, breathing through the hard parts, and saying to yourself, *"I'm still here—and I can meet life as I am, where I am."* It calls us to welcome *all* our selves—the younger selves who learned to protect us, the present selves who continue to seek balance, and the future selves still unfolding. Each carries wisdom that informs who we are becoming.

Dr. Crosbie Watler, RTT's lead psychiatrist, will speak to presence in more detail later; in short, it's a state of alert, non-judgmental awareness—meeting this moment *just as it is*. Presence interrupts automatic, fear-based reactions by anchoring us in the *here-and-now*. It steadies the nervous system, increases emotional regulation, and widens the space between stimulus and response. Practices that build our capacity for presence—like mindfulness and somatic awareness reduce reactivity, increase our psychological flexibility, and support our overall resilience and well-being (Goldberg et al., 2022).

This also doesn't mean we ignore pain or struggle. We acknowledge that life, trauma, and conditioning can disconnect us from our sense of wholeness.

But rather than approaching ourselves as problems to solve, we practice creating the inner and outer conditions where that wholeness can re-emerge.

Wholeness isn't about staying calm all the time—it's about noticing when we've wandered and finding our way back, like returning home after a long day. It grows each time we pause long enough to feel what's here, offer ourselves compassion, and take the next honest step. It's a living practice of meeting our inner experience without abandoning it.

For some, the idea of healing or wholeness may feel out of reach—especially when trauma has shaped a general sense of disconnection. Trust takes time. Move as slowly and gently as feels safe for you, trusting that every small step toward safety and connection is meaningful.

The practices you'll find here aren't prescriptions—they're invitations: reminders to pause, breathe, and return to what's steady beneath the noise of survival. As Wes Taylor—a member of our team that specializes in non-violent communication—often reminds us:

> We don't need fixing; we need reminding. When we truly see one another, something inside us wakes up—reminding us of who we are when we forget. For many of us, past wounds formed in the absence of this kind of presence; so, when it becomes available, healing becomes possible. What a powerful gift to offer another.

This is the essence of belonging. This piece by Toko-pa Turner (2017)—a Canadian author, poet, and dreamworker—reminds us of what belonging feels like when we stop trying to earn it. Her words speak to the parts of us that have longed to be seen, inviting us to remember ourselves home.

For the Misfits *by Toko-pa Turner*

For the rebels and the misfits, the black sheep and the outsiders. For the refugees, the orphans, the scapegoats, and the weirdos. For the uprooted, the abandoned, the shunned and invisible ones.

May you recognize with increasing vividness that you know what you know.

May you give up your allegiances to self-doubt, meekness, and hesitation.

May you be willing to be unlikable, and in the process be utterly loved.

May you be impervious to the wrongful projections of others, and may you deliver your disagreements with precision and grace.

May you see, with the consummate clarity of nature moving through you, that your voice is not only necessary, but desperately needed to sing us out of this muddle.

May you feel shored up, supported, entwined, and reassured as you offer yourself and your gifts to the world.

May you know for certain that even as you stand by yourself, you are not alone.

Turner's words remind us that belonging doesn't come from fitting in—it grows when the parts of ourselves that once hid for protection can return without condition.

Reclaiming Hidden Parts

When we override our limits—saying "yes" when we mean no, shelving our passions, or numbing hard feelings—it chips away at our sense of wholeness. These patterns aren't choices we make on purpose; they're protective responses, shaped by past experiences. Healing often begins when we feel ready to turn toward the parts of ourselves that had to retreat into the shadows to stay safe—not to fix them, but to offer enough safety for them to return to our awareness and the wholeness of who we are.

Emotions arise from different aspects of who we are. When a part of us is hurting, the emotion that comes with it is a signal—an invitation for awareness and care. When we can meet that emotion with presence, the part begins to reconnect and heal. When we can't, it may retreat until it feels safe again. The wound then takes on another form—what we might call *trauma*. When pain isn't compassionately witnessed, it doesn't disappear; it becomes stored in the body and nervous system. Over time, that unprocessed energy creates a kind of internal split within the self. The part remains but is held apart by the tension of what has yet to be integrated.

3

When we greet shame with compassion, the hidden parts of us begin to rise. Shame isn't our identity—it's a call for understanding. What once retreated into the dark often carries the very life we've been missing. These parts don't return to harm us—they return to be met and welcomed home.

Each time we turn toward an exiled part with curiosity instead of judgment, we begin to restore what once had to go underground for protection. In doing so, we bring movement to what was once frozen and invite the whole self back into connection. Our journey of healing is about remembering ourselves home.

Poet Robert Bly's metaphor of the long bag we drag behind us (1989) captures this beautifully. From childhood onward, we tuck away the parts of ourselves that felt like too much—too sensitive, too loud, too different. Over time, the bag grows heavy—not with burdens, but with the brilliance we once hid to stay safe.

Opening the bag isn't simple work. Those parts went into hiding for good reason; they need patience and safety to return. Healing isn't about emptying the bag all at once—it's about loosening what's been bound and inviting each piece to come back into the light at its own pace. These parts aren't broken; they've simply been waiting for the conditions where they can be seen, felt, and welcomed home.

Pause to Reflect: What's in your long bag?

Before you begin, remember this reflection isn't a demand—it's an invitation. This is where the *pace of trust* matters most. There's no need to dive deep or uncover everything at once. You might simply notice what arises, stay with it for a moment, and step back whenever you need to.

As you reflect, consider:

- What beliefs have shaped your sense of being 'enough'?
- Which parts of you feel distant yet call for your attention?
- What would it look like to welcome those parts—not to fix them, but to honour them?

This isn't about changing who we are—it's about remembering. What might we rediscover if we explore our long bag?

To meet what's been tucked away, we first need a foundation of inner security. Without it, our more vulnerable parts won't feel safe in our care. Healing asks us to re-parent ourselves in this way—to offer steady, compassionate presence to the parts that once had to hide for protection.

This is where resilience begins to take root—not through striving, but through alignment, meaning, and trust in our capacity to hold ourselves with care. As safety grows within and around us, we come to know what steadies us—the practices, connections, and perspectives that help us stay present when life becomes uncertain.

The Shape of Resilience

Resilience isn't simply about "bouncing back" or coping better in isolation. It is the ongoing capacity to stay in relationship—with all parts of ourselves, with others, and with life—especially in the presence of stress, uncertainty, and change. This capacity develops over time through lived experience, intentional practice, and supportive relationships. For this reason, we place a strong emphasis on community, presence, trustworthiness of relationships, and continuity of care rather than one-time interventions.

From this relational foundation, we can soften into the knowing that we are loved and accepted as we are, allowing our inner and outer worlds to align. This is the stable ground of **congruence** (Rogers, 1959).

When our roots are held by steady, well-resourced ground, a sense of stability naturally emerges. From this stability, we begin to trust that we can meet what comes—that even in uncertainty, we're going to be okay. This growing trust reflects what Antonovsky (1979) describes as a **sense of coherence**: the belief that life, even in its unpredictability, can be understood, managed, and held with meaning. From this place, we can extend our branches further into the world, guided by purpose and sustained by the resources that steady us.

These elements form the living shape of resilience—belonging and trust tethering us through connection and restoring balance. As shown in **Figure 1**, resilience is like a tree with deep roots: storms still come, but the roots hold, allowing us to bend, grow, and reach toward the light.

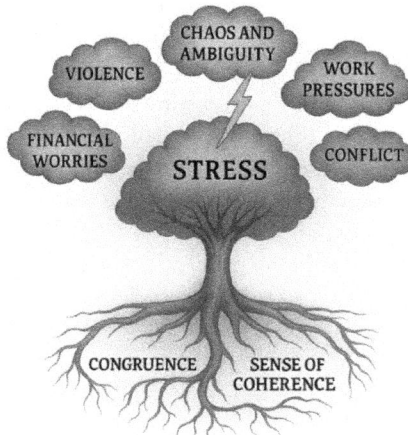

Figure 1. Congruence = Orientation to self; Sense of Coherence = Orientation to world.

Resilience *begins within us*, but it's *sustained between us*. We learn and grow through relationships marked by *presence* and *compassionate witnessing*. These relational dynamics are learned in practice—formed in everyday moments.

Congruence

Congruence is a key resilience factor and essential for wholeness. First described by Carl Rogers (1959), it reflects the alignment between our real and ideal selves—when who we are and how we show up are the same.

When we experience congruence, we move through life with integrity and ease. There's room for our full humanity—joy, grief, creativity, and confusion—all in the same space. It means setting the table for *all* parts of self to belong, to be seen, heard, and included in the conversation of the whole.

Sobonfu Somé, a respected spiritual teacher from Burkina Faso, describes a Dagara cultural practice that honours individuality from birth. In this tradition, pregnant women participate in a hearing ritual to discern the purpose of the incoming child, which informs both the child's name and their role in the community. Somé explains that a name carries its own energetic quality—one that shapes and shelters a person's life path (2004).

This teaching reminds us that belonging begins as a birthright, not a reward. When every part of us is welcome, there's no need to prove worthiness or hide for acceptance. Yet many of us were taught otherwise, learning to trade authenticity for safety.

The Cost of Disconnection

When belonging depends on approval, congruence begins to erode. Over time, a gap forms between who we truly are and who we think we need to be. This tension is illustrated in **Figure 2**. The heart, representing the real self, holds the belief that *I am enough as I am*, while the star, symbolizing the ideal self, holds the belief that *I am enough when I achieve enough*. Shame bridges the space between them, highlighting the emotional toll of striving to meet external standards. As the divide grows, so too does the burden of shame.

Shame grows when it's left alone. It spills into our relationships—sometimes as judgment, defensiveness, or trying to control, other times as withdrawal or self-criticism. When we lose connection with our inherent worth, it becomes difficult to see the worth in others. What begins as protection easily turns into projection, widening the very gap we most long to close (a dynamic we'll explore in the next Waypoint).

Figure 2. Congruence → the alignment between our real and ideal selves. The greater the divide between our real and ideal self, the more shame we carry.

Roots of Incongruence: Unmet needs

We draw here from Maslow's Hierarchy of Needs (1943), a framework that reminds us of the essential building blocks for human flourishing. When basic needs—such as nourishment, rest, and safety—are unmet, the nervous system prioritizes survival above all else. In this state, it becomes difficult to access the parts of ourselves that long for connection, creativity, or self-expression. Our energy is consumed by the immediate need to feel safe.

It's important to remember that *we can't heal what we can't afford to feel.* Before we can access deeper layers of authenticity, connection, and meaning, our most basic needs—physical, emotional, and relational—must be met. Safety is the soil from which every form of healing grows. Only when our environment and support systems allow it can our tender parts begin to surface and integrate.

As these foundational needs are met, our physiology starts to shift. The nervous system starts to settle, making room for curiosity, compassion, and connection. From that rooted sense of safety, we can reach toward love, belonging, purpose, and transcendence—the qualities that allow us not just to survive, but to thrive (**Figure 3**).

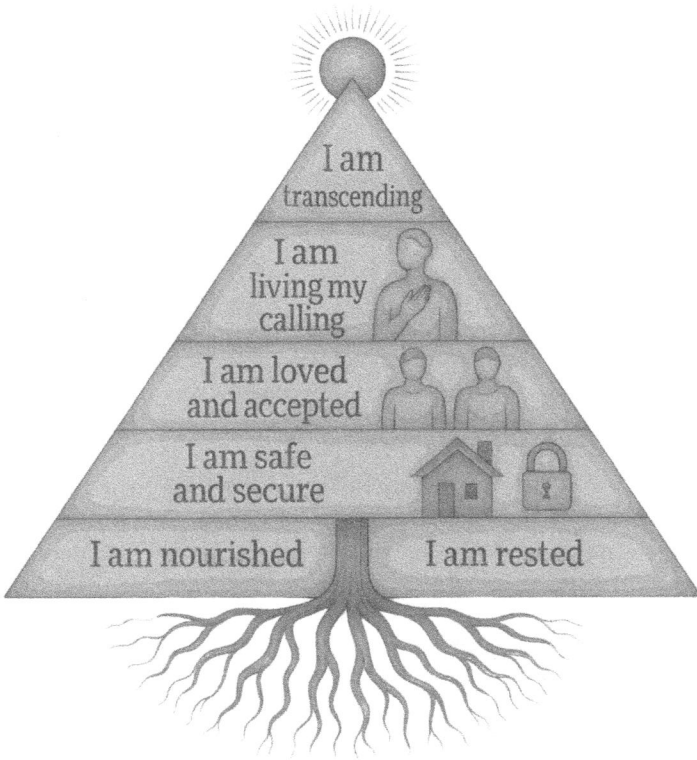

Figure 3. Maslow's description of basic human requirements correlates with the development of congruence and sense of coherence, representing aspects that are required for us to move from surviving to thriving.

Because acceptance and belonging are basic human needs, many of us learned early on to choose acceptance by others over authenticity. Picture a child who proudly calls herself an artist and is cheered on at first. But as she grows, the praise fades. The focus shifts to more practical things—like spelling, math, or getting good grades. Bit by bit, she learns that being accepted might mean hiding a part of herself.

She still loves to create, but the fear of rejection starts to take over. How others react to what she makes begins to matter more than the joy of creating itself. What begins as a small trade—belonging for authenticity—often becomes a lifelong equation:

DOing = Worth → DOing > BEing

Over time, these lessons shape how our nervous system responds to the world and how we see ourselves in it. We start to believe that some parts of us aren't safe to be visible. Incongruence takes hold—not from weakness, but as protection.

8

These survival patterns—self-silencing, people-pleasing, perfectionism, over-achieving, shrinking, or carefully monitoring others' reactions—are the adaptations our younger selves crafted to stay connected and safe. They are like roots that once grew toward survival.

From this steadier ground, we can notice old patterns, meeting them without judgment as we come to understand the conditions that shaped them. This awareness starts to show up in our behaviours, through a growing ability to be authentic, rather than hiding behind protective displays. For example, in moments of insecurity, instead of reacting, we pause and notice what's here: *a feeling of exposure, a guarding response, a part of us afraid to be seen.*

As we do this, we interrupt the old automatic loops. This noticing and nurturing creates space—turning what would have been a defensive reaction into a moment of connection, where we can compassionately witness ourselves and draw strength from those around us in our time of need, much like the roots of a forest—sharing nourishment and safety beneath the surface, receiving in times of need, and giving freely in times of plenty.

Each time we meet shame with curiosity, it creates more space for our inner world to meet the outer one. The roots that once tightened for protection begin to reach toward connection, drawing nourishment from belonging. Here, we remember that worth was never ours to earn—only ours to reclaim:

DOing ≠ Worth → BEing > DOing

As internal safety grows, striving to survive begins to ease. We can meet the world not from the pressure to prove, but from the freedom to live from our inherent worth. This is where self-kindness becomes possible—because to offer ourselves compassion, we must first believe we're worthy of it. Research supports this: when we relate to ourselves with kindness, the nervous system relaxes, perfectionism loosens its grip, and resilience takes root (Benedetto et al., 2024). As we learn to create this safe and kind inner space, our tender parts begin to re-appear—curious, playful, and creative—ready to rejoin the rhythm of our being.

This shift doesn't happen alone. We learn to live authentically through trust that grows in relationship. We stop hustling for worth when we feel seen, accepted, and supported as our whole selves. With time, the parts of us that once felt separate begin to come back into harmony again.

This is the essence of **unconditional positive regard**—the relational medicine that helps close the gap between who we are and who we've learned we need to be. When we are consistently met with acceptance—especially in our most vulnerable moments—we begin to trust our own *enoughness*. Over time, we embody that trust, and how we relate to ourselves and the world changes.

Unconditional Positive Regard (UPR)

The primary medicine in Roots to Thrive is *Unconditional Positive Regard (UPR)*—a concept introduced by psychologist Carl Rogers (1959) and a core requirement for congruence to emerge. UPR is the practice of accepting ourselves and others exactly as we are—without judgment or withdrawing care—even and especially when we make mistakes or show up imperfectly. It's grounded in the understanding that every part of us is doing the best it can with the tools available, shaped by our life experiences, resources, and capacities in any given moment.

UPR isn't something we master through logic or willpower. It's a felt sense of safety and worthiness that develops in relationships that consistently mirror it. We start to trust our inherent worth when we're met with genuine acceptance, especially in moments of vulnerability. This learning unfolds slowly, like learning a new rhythm that eventually becomes second nature.

As we embody UPR, we become able to welcome every part of ourselves into relationship—including the aspects that have been hidden, shamed, or silenced. These parts often approach with caution, needing to test whether they'll be met with care. When met with acceptance, trust begins to grow; when met with rejection, it erodes. In this way, vulnerability becomes the gateway to embodiment—a shift from knowing about safety to *actually* feeling it. Through integrating the parts once othered, we reclaim authenticity and return to wholeness.

This process is not solitary. It depends on being met by others who can hold that openness with steadiness and compassion—those who have learned the rhythm of UPR themselves and can offer a regulated presence that our nervous system can resonate with and settle beside.

For the parts of us that have felt like the misfits, scapegoats, or outsiders described earlier by Toko-pa Turner, this kind of presence is especially healing. It allows not only the once-hidden parts to emerge, but also the gifts those parts carry. In this way, UPR isn't just healing—it enables a radical shift, like opening a long-sealed door and inviting the parts once split-off for survival to finally come home. That opening is what makes thriving possible.

Research affirms that as we experience safety in our relationships, it grows our capacity to feel our worth, regulate our emotions, and remain resilient in the face of adversity (Surzykiewicz et al., 2022).

This process of healing through relationship isn't just emotional—it's biological. Our brains are wired for attunement and co-regulation—processes that make UPR both possible and powerful. Specialized cells called **mirror neurons** help us empathize and emotionally resonate with others (Bonini et al., 2022). They allow us to *feel with* each other—our brains lighting up in patterns like the people we're observing. Through these neural pathways, we literally *feel into* the emotional vibrations of those around us, learning their rhythm and beginning to **co-regulate** with them.

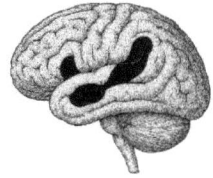

In cultures that prize conformity, we often learn to mirror what's acceptable rather than what's authentic. For many of us, UPR wasn't a steady presence in early life. Instead of being immersed in a consistent field of acceptance, we adapted to conditionality, tuning into others' expectations instead of our own truth. Over time, UPR becomes less of an innate state and more of a learned rhythm—one that must be reawakened through lived experience.

When we're in the presence of someone who embodies UPR, our nervous system begins to recalibrate through resonance and co-regulation. Mirror neurons play a vital role here, helping us internalize the experience of being accepted without condition. In this way, UPR becomes more than a concept—it's a living transmission, a relational energy passed from one regulated nervous system to another. Through presence, attunement, and **compassionate witnessing**, this transmission becomes a catalyst for transformation.

As we integrate this new way of being, our physiology shifts from reflexive defense to openness, from vigilance to trust. Over time, we learn to offer ourselves the same unconditional regard we once sought from others. This is the soil where authenticity grows—and where healing becomes embodied truth.

What does it look like to *embody* UPR?

- Freedom to express ourselves without fear of rejection
- Acceptance of mistakes as part of growth
- Celebrating differences rather than fearing them
- Respectful disagreement and openness to conflict
- Valuing process and progress over perfection
- Recognizing vulnerability as essential to connection
- Forming secure attachments with ourselves and others

If congruence reflects how we relate to ourselves and those who hold us, **sense of coherence** reflects how we relate to the world, helping us extend outward with purpose, meaning, and confidence.

Sense of Coherence

Sense of coherence supports our ability to extend our branches outward, allowing our gifts to express themselves in the world.

Coined by sociologist Aaron Antonovsky (1979), sense of coherence is an inner compass—a way of relating to life that improves our capacity to navigate what comes. Its three components—meaning, confidence, and understanding—form the foundation of our orientation, agency, and sense of purpose (**Figure 4**).

Antonovsky developed this framework through his research with Holocaust survivors, observing that even under extreme adversity, and despite similar external conditions, some individuals were able to sustain well-being while others experienced ongoing distress and *dis-ease*. The difference, he found, was not the absence of hardship, but the presence of this inner compass anchored in these three interrelated elements.

MEANING	CONFIDENCE	UNDERSTANDING
What I am doing matters	I have what it takes	Life makes sense

Figure 4. Together, these three elements strengthen our sense of agency—empowering us to meet life's challenges with perspective and purpose—and serve as a buffer against stress.

Understanding helps us make sense of what's happening, creating a sense of predictability and manageability in our lives. *Confidence* grows from trusting our inner and outer resources to meet life's demands. *Meaning* gives us the courage to face the tough times and can even help us see challenges as opportunities to learn and grow.

Agency is then our felt sense of choice and participation in life—the understanding that, even with uncertainty, we can meet what comes our way. It grows when we feel safe enough to make decisions, take small steps, and see the impact of our actions.

Together, these elements shape our capacity to meet life as it unfolds, and to trust in our ability to respond to life rather than react to it.

Sense of coherence isn't a fixed state; it ebbs and flows with life's circumstances. When it weakens, we're more likely to see challenges as threats, activating the body's stress response and narrowing our perspective. During periods of heightened stress (explored further in the next Waypoint), our reactions can bypass awareness altogether, leaving us feeling reactive or ashamed afterward. Recognizing that these responses arise from survival, not failure, allows us to meet ourselves with compassion and reclaim a sense of agency—expanding the choices available to us as we face adversity.

This orientation is mirrored neurologically too: as our sense of coherence grows, the nervous system begins to trust in our resources, making it less likely to react when challenges arise. The body relaxes, the mind opens, and regulation becomes more fluid and adaptive. The anterior cingulate cortex (ACC)—a region located in both hemispheres of the brain— plays a pivotal role in this process. Research shows that the ACC activates when we choose to do something difficult because it aligns with our values (Touroutoglou et al., 2020). Through this alignment between action and inner truth, neural pathways are rewired—strengthening our belief that we can meet life's demands and find meaning within them. Essentially, the ACC helps develop an inner knowing that sounds like this: *This makes sense. This matters to me. And I've got this.*

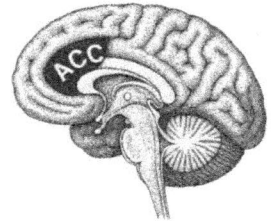

As we grow in trust, sense of coherence becomes less about control and more about faith—an embodied knowing that even with uncertainty, life can still be met with steadiness and care. Cultivating this sense of coherence allows us to face adversity with perspective and grace. It helps us remain open to meaning in hardship and connected to purpose even when the path ahead is unclear.

As our sense of coherence grows, this inner trust starts to extend outward, enabling safety to be lived out and reinforced through relationships. Our inner and outer worlds begin to intertwine—each shaping and strengthening the other.

Intertwining Root Systems: Nutrition for our nervous systems

This collective healing isn't metaphorical—it's biological. Safe, attuned relationships have the power to calm the nervous system, reducing reactivity and impulsive responses (**Figure 5**). Think of it as tuning into a steady frequency. When we're anxious or dysregulated, our internal signal becomes erratic. But in the presence of someone grounded and accepting, our nervous system begins to sync with theirs—like adjusting a radio to a clearer station.

This is the essence of **co-regulation**. Much like a tree extending its roots deep into the earth, connection with others who embody safety and presence helps us feel more grounded and secure. These relational roots protect us from external stressors and remind us that we don't have to carry the "long bag," as Robert Bly described, alone. Healing unfolds not in isolation but in the presence of compassionate others who, simply by walking beside us, help lighten the load.

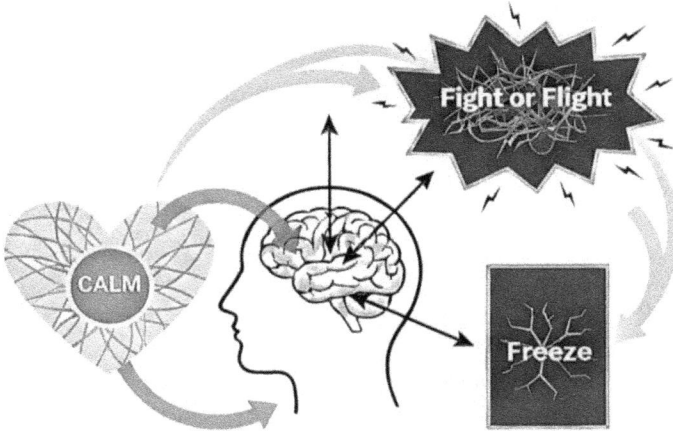

Figure 5. Relationships grounded in unconditional positive regard help us feel safe, calming the nervous system, so it isn't driving our behaviours.

Over time, these experiences begin to *rewire the brain*, forming new neural pathways that help us **regulate**—providing the ability to stay present and responsive to the emotions and sensations that arise in the body.

As our nervous system learns what safety feels like, we can meet difficult moments without being overwhelmed. Instead of being pulled into old protective patterns, we notice and tend to the unmet needs beneath our reactions. The strongest source of this steadiness is connection and a felt sense of belonging—knowing we're not alone. This shift from reactivity to responsiveness marks a real turning point in the move from *surviving to thriving*.

As relationships deepen and trust grows, the impulse to perform, please, or protect begins to ease. We learn to offer ourselves the same kindness we receive from others, and this internalized compassion becomes a steadying force—an anchor we can return to in times of stress.

And perhaps even more important than what we *do* is *how we show up*—and *who we show up beside*. Our presence—calm, attuned, and grounded—shapes how others feel and how their bodies respond. It's the grounding medicine our beloved pet provides by simply walking into the room—no words required.

Attuned presence can shift mood and biological stress markers such as cortisol and salivary alpha-amylase (Battaglini et al., 2025). Neuroscience also demonstrates that our brains mirror the emotions of those around us (Bekkali et al., 2021). This helps explain why grounded energy can soothe, while tension or fear can ripple outward.

Showing up as a compassionate witness is a subtle yet powerful medicine. It asks only that we arrive authentically and stay present with *what is*.

In RTT, relationship extends beyond human connection. For example, rosemary often accompanies our practices as a grounding ally, its scent drawing us back into the body and reminding us of the land's maternal nature. Indigenous teachings affirm that tending relationships with the living world is an act of reconciliation and, ultimately, healing—reconnecting us to ancestral knowledge and deepening our sense of belonging (Joseph, 2021). When we include the more-than-human world in all our relations—plants, animals, water, sky, and soil—we expand our community of practice and the supports available to us.

For resilience to shift from a concept into lived experience, we must "toddler" our way through it—learning by doing, experimenting, and returning again and again in the communities we practice in.

Communities of Practice (CoP)

In RTT, *Communities of Practice (CoPs)* are relational containers designed to foster safety, trust, and transformation. Their foundation is built on **shared intentions and agreements**—not just guidelines, but living commitments that shape how we show up together. Like the roots of a tree, these elements intertwine beneath the surface, creating stability and resilience when challenges show up.

Shared Intentions act as a North Star, guiding the group toward a common purpose. When held collectively, they amplify alignment and ease, allowing the group to move in rhythm.

Agreements provide the structure that holds us steady—threads of mutual understanding that support transparency, predictability, and that make trust possible. Together, they reduce anxiety and create the conditions where vulnerability, authenticity, and connection can take root.

When we live in alignment with our intentions and agreements, the group moves with flow. When we fall out of alignment, it's like an instrument slipping out of tune—discord arises, and the whole song of the community feels off beat.

At the heart of every CoP is presence—animated through unconditional positive regard and compassionate witnessing. It's not about perfection but about *showing up as we are*. Consistency in this context doesn't mean that we never wobble; it means we know how to lean into our resources and into one another when we do.

Even imperfect presence—when offered with sincerity—creates a field of safety. When we soak in presence held with unconditional positive regard and compassionate witnessing, it becomes a medicine for healing—expanding our capacity for secure attachment (explored further in *Waypoint 8*). This kind of presence builds trust, allowing us to feel truly seen and supported.

Crosbie speaks to the power of presence and service in community:

> As mentioned earlier, *presence* refers to a state of alert, non-judgmental, present-moment awareness. This creates a safe and grounded space, where others can lean in, reconnecting with their true nature and inner knowing. We have simply become the reminder.
>
> We no longer feel the need to fix, understanding that our grounded attention is the most precious gift we can give. Practiced with shared intention, this way of relating creates a safe container for our conversations. What matters most is not the content of our words, but the awareness behind them—if we choose to speak at all.

How CoPs Shape the Resilient Brain

These relational practices are not just helpful — they're essential. They move unconditional positive regard from something we understand cognitively to something we embody. And embodiment takes practice, which is why CoPs are vital. They are more than support groups; they are *living laboratories* where we learn to co-regulate, to witness and be witnessed with compassion, and to cultivate safety, trust, and authenticity as everyday behaviours rather than abstract ideals.

As we mentioned earlier, our nervous system gives us a real, biological sign of resilience in action. As shown in **Figure 6**, genuine connection activates the mirror-neuron system, which helps us *tune in* to others and feel *with* them (Bonini et al., 2022). Likewise, practicing vulnerability in safe relational space expands our window of tolerance and engages the anterior cingulate cortex (ACC), which helps us stay with discomfort, regulate emotions, and act in alignment with our values (Touroutoglou et al., 2020). Together, these relational–neural processes reflect the inner work of congruence and sense of coherence, forming the biological foundation for the resilience we cultivate in community.

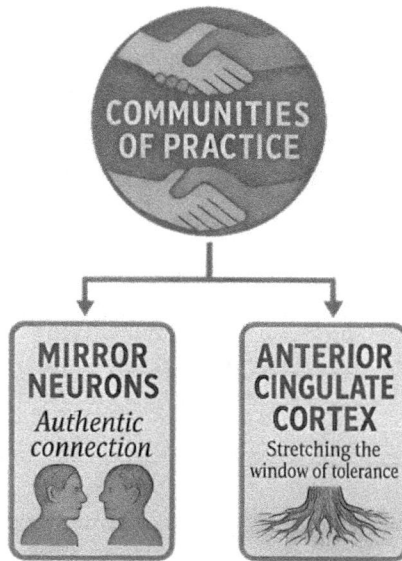

Figure 6. Predictable environments and compassionate witnessing activate brain systems—mirror neurons and the ACC—that support emotional regulation and authentic connection.

The spirit of the CoP doesn't end with the program. These relational ways of being are meant to carry into our families, friendships, workplaces, and broader communities. By building intentional, supportive relationships rooted in shared intentions and agreements, we extend the safety of the CoP into daily life.

Our relationships then become real places of practice — spaces where we can show up honestly, care for one another, and strengthen our capacity for congruence and sense of coherence. To honour this, RTT offers dedicated sessions for family and friends, inviting loved ones to engage as fellow travellers and helping bring the principles of unconditional positive regard and co-regulation into the wider circle of our lives.

Pause to Reflect: Who helps you feel emotionally safe?

When the conditions for safety are present—through shared intentions, agreements, and attuned presence—something powerful begins to unfold. We feel more able to show up authentically, and less compelled to perform or protect. But emotional safety isn't just a group experience—it's also shaped by the relationships we carry with us.

Take a moment to reflect on your current relationships and notice how they make you feel. As you explore these feelings, identify where unconditional positive regard already shows up—and where it might be missing or ready to grow.

- Where and with whom do you feel most self-conscious?
- Where and with whom do you feel most free?
- Who can you be completely honest with, without fear of rejection?

These reflections help reveal the people who anchor you in self-trust—the ones who meet you with presence rather than performance.

Pause to Practice: 'Checking in' and buddies

In RTT CoPs, the small-group session begins with a check-in—a simple yet powerful ritual of connection. Each member names one or two bodily sensations and one or two emotions, without analyzing or explaining. For example, instead of saying *I'm tired*, one might say, *I feel a dull heaviness in my shoulders.* This helps us connect somatically and builds emotional literacy.

Let's practice. What sensations and emotions are present right now? No need to act or judge. Just witness what's arising.

In addition to group check-ins, participants are paired with a buddy in the first week of the program. Buddies connect weekly—by phone, text, online, or in person—for 5 to 15 minutes. This brief ritual offers a consistent opportunity to practice checking in, giving and receiving unconditional positive regard, and witnessing with compassion.

If you're engaging with this work outside of RTT, consider forming your own circle or inviting a travelling companion—someone who shares your intentions and values. Even brief, intentional conversations can offer support, perspective, and remind us that we don't have to walk this path alone.

Whether in your CoP or with your buddy, a simple check-in might include:

- **Quick Check-In:** Share 1-2 physical sensations and 1-2 emotions.
- **Deeper Check-In:** Each person responds to a guiding question by noticing any new or shifting sensations or emotions, without diving into the story behind them.
- **Quick Check-Out:** Repeat 1-2 sensations and emotions, observing any changes since your first check-in.

These practices help transition insight from something we name and understand into something we feel and live. They stretch our comfort zones and soften the grip of fear and self-protection. Over time, they cultivate trust, compassion, and a sense of authenticity—within ourselves and in our relationships.

Through the mirror of relationship, we start to see the stories we've been living—beliefs about our worth and our place that shape our reactions and patterns. Todd's offering below helps us soften our attachment to old narratives, making space for something new emerge.

Working with our Narrative/Story
by Todd Haspect, senior therapist & facilitator

One of the general themes we collectively work with in your community of practice (CoP) is the concept of staying out of **story** (or *narrative* if that lands better for you). Our stories matter, but their usefulness in healing is limited. *Story* typically keeps us in our heads and focused on the past. Research shows that when we learn to step out of repetitive, negative thinking patterns—like rumination—we often feel less anxious or depressed and more emotionally balanced (Hasani et al., 2025).

Staying present and dropping our focus into the body are two key practices we work on in our time together. These practices are meant to guide our check-ins, check-outs, and compassionate witnessing, which is covered in more detail in the first CoP. I am inviting us all to lean into this.

Whether we are responding to a weekly question or offering compassionate witnessing, it's normal to be pulled into our familiar stories. This is often connected to the patterns we want to shift in ourselves and so is valuable to notice. When we find stories popping up as we listen or respond, we pay attention to what our bodies tell us about this.

This way of relating takes practice. As you grow in your process, a CoP facilitator might gently prompt you with something like: *I noticed you were pulled into story—this seems important. As you were speaking, what did you notice below the neck?* As we notice how the age-old stories we carry shape our patterned behaviours, the potential for new stories becomes possible.

Service: The full circle of giving and receiving

Earlier, Crosbie spoke to the power of presence. Service can then be understood as *presence in action*—the natural overflow of a grounded, grateful heart. As trust deepens and our practice matures, what we cultivate in our Communities of Practice begins to infuse our wider relationships. Presence becomes less a technique and more a way of being, bringing us to the heart of our shared work: *showing up in service.*

From this centered place, service doesn't arise from intellect or expertise but from gratitude. Like a full cup that naturally overflows, it extends outward without ego, agenda, or attachment to outcomes. When healing takes root, this way of showing up becomes a natural expression of our security and wellness—*not an effortful task.* Research backs this up. Everyday acts of kindness and support increase our sense of well-being, confidence, and meaning, making service something that grows out of flourishing rather than obligation (Rowland & Curry, 2019). Gratitude strengthens this even more. When people genuinely feel grateful on a regular basis, they're more likely to help others—suggesting that service becomes a natural extension of how we feel inside (Zhu et al., 2024).

So, our capacity for gratitude—and the ripple effect of service that grows from it—is influenced far more by our inner landscape than by external circumstances, even if it doesn't always feel that way. The patterns we struggle with around us often reflect what's seeking healing within us. These unconscious loops—old thoughts, emotional reactions, and protective habits—narrow our presence until they're brought into awareness. Jung (1959) suggested that the inner dynamics we leave unexamined inevitably surface in our external relationships. Even when the people in our lives change, familiar painful patterns often stay the same. They tend to repeat until we feel secure enough to recognize the distortion for what it is—*an old protective story*—and resourced enough to shift it rather than get pulled back into it.

Recognizing this, healing begins by *remembering our wholeness* and then *noticing what obscures it*—the stories, beliefs, and relational patterns that cycle through familiar themes. These repeating dynamics signal aspects of ourselves asking for attention and reintegration. Without awareness, disconnection tends to persist, only taking new shapes in our lives.

When we bring these hidden dynamics into the light, we begin to resource ourselves in ways that allow us to respond rather than react. Healing becomes less about fixing and more about remembering our inner resources, meeting recurring patterns with curiosity and compassion. As awareness grows, choices appear where reactions once lived (London et al., 2023). In time, the very patterns that once disrupted us become our teachers.

To guide us further along this path, Crosbie offers insight into the common patterns that create suffering and ways to work compassionately with them.

A Mindful Path: Patterns that create suffering
by Dr. Crosbie Watler, lead psychiatrist

Much like inclement weather, challenges come and go, often unexpected and often outside our control. Challenges can activate reactive patterns of judgment and resistance, where our true nature is eclipsed by the mind field. The mind's sole purpose is to think, to turn. The mind is a good servant, but a poor master (Wallace, 2009).

We are called to bring discernment to our thought patterns, like the acronym W.A.I.T.—*Why am I thinking? Is it serving any purpose, or simply crowding space?*

Our true nature is simply awareness without thought. True nature resides in the space between our thoughts. Research shows that intentionally pausing in this space, through present-moment attention and nonjudgmental awareness, can reduce rumination and enhance focus and emotional well-being (Blanke et al., 2020).

Thoughts come and go, but I am not the thinker—I am the witness of thought. Exploding the myth of *I think, therefore, I am* to simply *I am*—no condition. No one and nothing outside of me is required to complete me

When we look externally for our worth, the *doings* are never enough, and we are never enough. Our thoughts and emotions often create an escalating body-mind activation, keeping us stuck in self-defeating patterns. Our thoughts and emotions are literal gas guzzlers, consuming all our attention, and eclipsing the still awareness of true nature: the *being* self. Metaphorically, the clouds have obscured the sun. We then believe that we are the clouds, the veneer, not the essence of the thing. Yet, the sun has never gone away, always present, patiently waiting for a crack in the facade to reveal herself. Even on the darkest day.

We are called to notice when the mind is driving the bus, and the distress that usually ensues: *Am I using my mind, or is my mind using me?* Our bodies will tell us—constriction, tension, heaviness. No need to name the emotion or the story connected to it. No need to push it away. Rather, we cultivate a practice of noticing when we lose it to the stickiness of the mind field and return to true nature.

We connect with our true nature, being self, not by resisting thought, but by stepping out of thought. Here, we can trust the truth that awareness can only be in one place at a time. Anchoring 100% of our attention to the flow of breath in and down, and up and out, bringing awareness to the flow of breath and the space it creates in our bodies. Bringing our awareness from above the neck to below the neck, using breath as our trustworthy ally.

To ward off insecurity and the *need* to know, the mind/ego will put everything into little boxes, manufacturing 'truths' that ain't necessarily so. Here is a familiar theme: *I am not enough; I am a failure.*

That narrative lands hard, and we've all been there, needing something out there to complete us. A success, a validation, a relationship, seeking to arrive at some future moment that's better than the present moment. When we succeed at any given enterprise, our happiness is transient and conditional. In truth, we have outsourced our well-being to the weather of our lives.

I shame or blame myself. Or, to avoid awareness of any cracks in my own facade, I project anger or judgment onto others…again, *who is angry with whom?* My insecure toddler self conflicts with your insecure toddler self, and if we relate from there, we both lose.

What if we bring curiosity to our stuck thought patterns: *Who is not enough, who is the I that's a failure?*

Our doing selves will never be enough. The *DOing* self is a perpetual toddler, doing the best we can with our awareness and tools at any point in time. We do not shame a toddler for her missteps. We understand that the toddler is doing the best she can with her awareness and tools. The toddler can simply do no better; it's not a choice, and there is no shame in it.

When the mind's addiction pulls us up and out, we are invited to notice: *How grounded am I?* Our bodies will always tell us when we've drifted away—just as our awareness will. The goal isn't to never lose our center, but to return, again and again, to still awareness.

As Elder Duncan Grady (personal communication, March 2023) reminds us, *"better to go in and down, than up and out, though the latter is far more seductive."*

The breath becomes a faithful ally in this practice—a tether to our true nature and to the wisdom that lives in the space between thoughts.

The deepest thinkers think very little; they cultivate still awareness, bringing wisdom and discernment to the task at hand. My highest purpose is no longer what *I do*; it's noticing when my mind is stuck in the habitual field that creates suffering, redirecting to the creative field of still awareness.

In that space, there is no judgment of self or others, no scarcity of attachment—only gratitude and compassion. We don't choose our patterns, and we all have patterns that don't serve. Our doing/toddler self is doing the best it can. Others too. True nature can leave the light on, holding space for compassion and unconditional positive regard.

Despite my lying eyes telling me I'm all grown up, I've surrendered to the fact that my doing self is a perpetual toddler, and that it's not a matter of if, but a matter of when, I'll fall on my ass. At those times, I am called to notice; to align with true nature, bringing awareness to missteps and patterns that do not serve. With time, we come to know and trust the healing and wisdom that greets us in the space between our thoughts. It is, after all, our birthright; the clouds just got in the way.

The Inner Flame

Over time, rather than striving to become something different, we find ourselves softening, meeting our missteps with gentleness and returning to what matters with more curiosity than urgency. As we do, the rigid patterns that once drove reactive behaviour begin to loosen, making space for something more spacious and authentic to emerge.

Beneath the noise of constant doing, a quieter knowing waits patiently—a spark that glows even when forgotten. One participant described this beautifully: *"You start at your darkness and work your way back to your own light."*

In RTT, Elder Geraldine Manson often refers to this spark as the **pilot light**—a small but unwavering flame at the centre of our being. Her teaching reminds us that tending this flame begins with remembering our inherent wholeness. Every part of us, even those that hid or hardened for survival, is worthy of returning to the light.

When we lose connection with parts of ourselves, the flame can feel dimmed. These inner distances often began as protection—moments when turning away from pain felt safer than staying with it. Over time, these disconnections can solidify into patterns that leave us feeling scattered or incomplete. In RTT, we name this not as brokenness but as fragmentation born from pain that occurred without a compassionate witness. These returning parts need compassion, not correction.

RTT senior facilitator Julia Sheffield reminds us of a foundational truth: *Not broken. Never was.* This remembering is the heart of the work, the slow and steady welcoming of the pieces of us that have been waiting for warmth.

The **Japanese art of Kintsugi** offers a powerful metaphor for this reclamation (Olivetti, 2023). Rather than hiding cracks in broken pottery, Kintsugi repairs them with gold, honouring the vessel's history. Nothing is concealed or discarded. What once seemed broken becomes a new expression of beauty—defined by resilience rather than perfection.

The following poem—rendered by Daniel Ladinsky (2002) from the poetry of Ḥāfez (1315–1390 CE)—speaks to the same truth:
that beneath all conditioning, striving, and self-doubt, there is a light that has never gone out.

The Seed of Your Heart

Every part of you
has a secret language.
Your heart,
when it finally speaks,
will tell you:
"I am made of light."
Listen,
and you will know
you were never meant to be less
than whole.

Each act of awareness—each mindful breath—is an offering to this flame, reminding us that the light was never lost. From this steadier place, we meet life's challenges with greater trust and flexibility. This is the essence of resilience: the capacity to return to balance even when life feels uncertain. Resilience doesn't replace our wholeness; it gives us access to it.

Being true to ourselves can stir fear—especially the fear of rejection or misunderstanding. When safety feels out of reach, we may shut down or retreat into overthinking. This is why healing must include the body, using trauma-informed practices that honour the nervous system's need for safety (Nguyen Feng et al., 2025; Lynch et al., 2025). From this grounded place, emotions become messengers rather than problems—signals of stress, unmet needs, or perceived danger (Greenberg & Goldman, 2019). As inner harmony grows, our capacity for authentic connection grows with it (Querdasi & Callaghan, 2023).

Finding your own rhythm is essential. When people feel supported and allowed to move at a pace that feels right for them, their ability to recover from trauma increases significantly (Grass et al., 2025). These moments teach us boundaries, self-kindness, and the resilience that develops through self-awareness. As we learn to meet discomfort with steadiness, we gain the courage to ask for help, receive support, and move forward with confidence.

As we close this chapter, remember that healing isn't a destination but a lived practice—more rhythmic than linear. It invites us to return, again and again, to presence, compassion, and the steady unfolding of who we are becoming.

From this foundation, we're invited to deepen our roots, reconnect with our inner flame, and explore what it truly means to thrive—not through perfection or performance, but through *awareness, regulation, compassion*, and *alignment* with our true nature.

In the pages ahead, we turn toward the four core practices that help cultivate these roots and support congruence and a sense of coherence. Each practice includes written guidance, along with optional short videos accessible through QR codes for those who prefer a different format.

Awareness: Remembering our true self and the resources within and around us.

Who am I, and what are my resources?

Regulation: Attuning to supportive rhythms—within the body, in community, and through meaningful action that restores agency.

What helps me feel safe and secure?

Compassion: Offering unconditional care to self and others—heart-fullness in action.

What helps me embody unconditional positive regard?

Alignment: Rediscovering an inner compass and the integrity to live our calling.

What matters to me?

Each of these practices, illustrated in **Figure 7**, is woven throughout the RTT framework—linking theory with lived experience. Like roots, branches, and fruits, they reflect the ongoing process of growth, integration, and embodiment, preparing us to face life's storms with greater resilience.

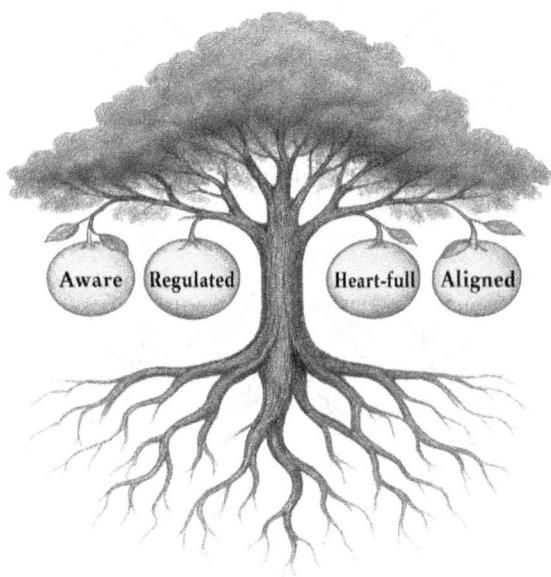

Figure 7. The Tree of Resilience: roots as inner strengths, branches as external supports, fruits as embodied contributions.

A Note About Repeating & Returning

As you move through the Waypoints, you'll notice that core teachings and practices show up more than once, even several times. This is intentional. The nervous system learns the way the land does—through familiar rhythms of return. A practice introduced early may meet you differently later, when another part of you has surfaced and is ready to receive it. For this reason, you'll see the foundational roots of resilience (**Figure 7**) and core practices to help develop them, woven through multiple Waypoints. These returns are invitations, not lessons to memorize—more like circling a sacred teaching from a new angle, each encounter offering a fresh way to listen.

This orientation toward returning reminds us that resilience isn't static. It grows through familiarity in relationship. Just as a tree depends on the quality of its soil and the wider ecosystem, our growth is shaped by the environments, people, and practices we immerse in.

With these foundations in place, we turn to what tests them: **stress**—our relationship to it, how it moves through the body, and how, in its own way, it calls us to return, to who we are and the resources available to us.

WAYPOINT 2: DEVELOPING ROOTS TO THRIVE

Understanding the Roots of Stress

Stress isn't weakness—it's protection. Sometimes it keeps us safe; sometimes it reveals old wounds asking to be healed.

Imagine an ocean with towering waves. With a board and the skills to ride, it's exhilarating. Without tools—or when fear takes over—the same waves feel threatening. The waves don't change; our relationship to them does.

A Surfer's Lens

Sense of Coherence = The Board

Your ability to make sense of the world, trust your capacity, and find meaning. A sturdy *board* helps you respond with intention, even in rough water.

Congruence = Your Stance

How you show up—grounded, authentic, emotionally honest. A steady stance keeps you connected to your inner compass when the sea gets choppy.

Together, board and stance enable you to ride the waves with purpose and confidence.

As Crystal Fee, a senior nurse on our team, reminds us: *"Like crystals forming in the cracks, strength and beauty emerge not from brokenness, but from the spaces life has stretched us open."*

These words echo a truth found in research: growth often arises *because of* adversity, not despite it (Tedeschi & Calhoun, 2004). To harness that growth, we first need to look beneath the surface—to the body's natural intelligence. Understanding how stress shapes our thoughts, emotions, and relationships begins here, in the rhythms of the nervous system. Physiology tells the story of how protection begins and, when unchecked, how it can become *over*protection.

The Physiology of Stress

Stress happens when the nervous system detects a *potential* threat to our needs. The brain signals the body, and a full-system response engages in an instant— faster than conscious thought—because speed can save us. Our survival can depend on it. This rapid pattern is the **stress response** (see **Figure 8**).

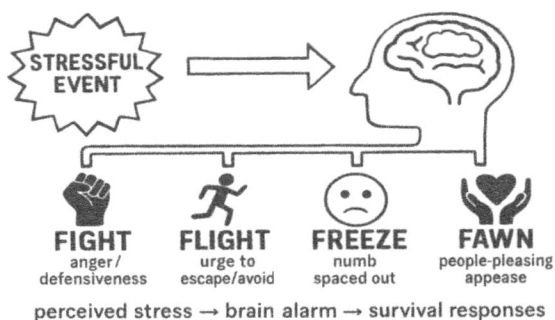

Figure 8. Stressful moments can activate survival responses—fight, flight, freeze, or fawn—as the body tries to protect us, even when the threat isn't real.

The stress response is adaptive: it sharpens focus, fuels action and protects us in moments of danger. But when stress becomes chronic, this same system can begin to work against us. Instead of helping us respond, it traps the body in a state of reactivity.

For example, imagine driving home from a funeral when a car suddenly swerves in front of you. In an instant, your grief is replaced by a surge of adrenaline as your focus narrows to the road. Your body has temporarily set aside emotion to prioritize safety. Once the threat has passed, the system can return to processing grief.

The same protective reflex can arise when our own emotions feel unsafe. The body steps back from those feelings—not because we're choosing to avoid them, but because, in that moment, it doesn't yet feel safe enough to stay with what's there. Over time, these protective patterns can become habitual, leaving us feeling stuck or disconnected from ourselves and others.

Understanding how stress works in the body is only part of the picture. The next reflection opens space for us to explore how stress feels and functions in our own experience.

Pause to Reflect: What's stress to you?

Stress is part of being human. Yet the way we experience it—and the meaning we make of it—shapes whether it becomes a source of growth or suffering. Take a moment to notice your own relationship with stress:

- What's stress to you—a signal, a threat, or something else?
- What typically activates your stress response?
- How does stress show up in your body?
- Which pattern arises most often for you: fight, flee, freeze, or fawn?
- When has stress helped you?
- When has stress led you to act out of alignment with your values?

28

The practices here are a small selection of simple tools our team has come to trust—and that participants often find themselves returning to. There's no pressure to master them all. What matters is finding what resonates—methods that help you feel grounded, not obligated. Experiment with curiosity; keep what supports you and release what doesn't.

The following practices are introduced more fully in later Waypoints. Each supports the nervous system's natural capacity to regulate and restore safety:

- **R.A.I.N.S.** - mindfulness-based self-compassion in action
- **4–7–8 Breath** - parasympathetic activation
- **Comforting Touch** - self-contact for grounding
- **The Butterfly Hug** - bilateral stimulation for regulation
- **EFT (Emotional Freedom Technique)** - tapping on acupressure points to release tension.

We introduce them briefly here in case you feel called to explore them more deeply at this stage; their full descriptions can be found in the Table of Contents. These practices are foundational in RTT's communities of practice, helping us to stay present, regulated, and connected as we navigate personal and collective challenges.

Awareness of our stress response gives us a clearer view of the inner weather that's shaping our moods and behaviours. Just as a tree withstands changing seasons through the strength of its roots, we too can cultivate stability and resilience beneath life's storms.

Rooted Enough to Weather the Weather

Returning to the tree metaphor, those with strong roots—developed through congruence and a sense of coherence—can weather emotional storms with greater stability. Stressful events are like changing weather; they get our attention but don't define the climate.

For instance, the thought of an upcoming exam might activate anxiety, even though the event isn't happening yet. If you feel prepared and supported, that same anticipation can energize you. The difference lies in perception: whether we interpret a challenge as a threat or an opportunity.

Like trees, we grow in ecosystems that both nourish and challenge us— conditions that inform our becoming. Some of our roots have been developed in **toxic soils**—systems shaped by colonialism and oppression. Overt and subtle forms of racism and discrimination keep the nervous system on alert, creating a constant sense of threat—especially when they invalidate or silence parts of our identity. Relief often comes from a blend of outer change— addressing unsafe environments—*and* inner skills—resourcing, community, and self-compassion. Strengthening ties with people who truly see you, and asking for support when you feel unsafe, expands capacity and reduces harm.

With deep roots, everyday threats are less likely to become chronic stressors. Without these basic safety requirements, thriving is compromised. This is why healing can't be separated from justice, nor personal regulation from relational safety. Both are needed for resilience to take root.

Understanding that we *can't* control the weather, but we *can* cultivate strong roots, shifts how we relate to challenge. The following practice by Crosbie offers a way to bring this understanding into lived experience.

Storm Watching with Non-Attachment
by Dr. Crosbie Watler, lead psychiatrist

Challenges are objective events in the external domain. Many challenges are outside our ability to directly predict or control outcomes. We create problems when we fixate on outcomes when all we control is process. The student can worry about the outcome of an exam *or* commit to a process of study.

Many of life's challenges are process challenges—examples include health, relationships, and financial planning. With each challenge, we need to identify whether we control the outcome directly or process only. We can then redirect our full attention to the process, detaching from outcomes we do not directly control. Not surprisingly, we do better.

This is the foundation of sport psychology, where the elite athlete commits to a process of training and preparation. On game day, the athlete steps on the field of play, grounded in present moment awareness, redirecting from any attachment to outcome. Free from anticipatory worry, the athlete's finite capacity for attention is right here, right now, the only place where she has agency.

Challenges and emotions come and go, like the weather, but we are not the weather. When it rains, we don't say I am the rain, rather, I observe the rain. I am not that; I am the observer. There is space. When we storm watch from a safe, secure space, the weather of our emotions might not change, but we have changed our relationship with it.

Pause for a moment and consider the contrasting experiences of witnessing passing weather events as an observer, versus feeling adrift and vulnerable amidst them. To adopt the perspective of an observer, engage in mindfulness, which is an intentional focus on the present moment with a sense of detachment. In doing so, we connect to who is paying attention (this is you, as the observer). *Who is the witness of this moment? Who am I?*

Our enduring and essential quality is awareness without thought. Some call it consciousness, the non-verbal stillness of being, nothing else required. We are already whole. In that space, we don't mind what happens, and challenges become opportunities for noticing when we lose it and are called to return to true nature.

Breath can guide us there, shifting our attention, *on purpose*, from above the neck to below the neck. With attention, follow the breath in and down to notice the inner space of the body. When we lose this awareness, when our mind starts to think, *what have we lost*? Simply space, that grounded felt sense of the space between our thoughts, where who we really are resides.

Non-Attachment: Stepping back from the flames

Crosbie describes non-attachment as the practice of creating space between ourselves and our emotional "weather," allowing us to observe what's happening without being pulled into it. This perspective captures the essence of **non-attachment**: stepping back from outcomes and emotional storms so we can stay rooted in the part of us that *notices* rather than *reacts*.

Non-attachment doesn't mean suppressing emotion or pulling away from life, it means relating to our experience from a steadier inner place. Research shows that this kind of spacious awareness builds psychological flexibility, helping us stay clear-minded even in moments of strong emotion (Tremblay et al., 2024).

Creating even a small amount of distance from emotional heat—like the lowered match in **Figure 9**—gives us room to choose our response instead of reacting automatically and getting burned in the process. Stepping back isn't avoidance; it's protection from overwhelm, allowing us to meet what's happening with clarity and compassion rather than reacting in ways that let harm move through us and into our relationships.

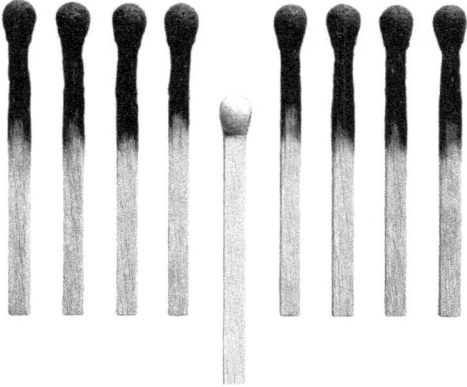

Figure 9. Creating space from what feels threatening helps prevent reactive stress responses and supports compassionate engagement.

When there is space around our emotions, we are more able to notice old patterns resurfacing. Often, what feels like a strong reaction to the present is connected to something that happened long ago. Understanding this helps us meet our emotions with tenderness rather than judgment—an invitation to care for the parts of us still carrying old pain.

Present Day Stress or the Echo of a Past Wound?

Trauma isn't defined by what happened to us—it's shaped by whether we feel safe enough to meet the feelings that came with it. When emotions go unexpressed, the energy of those moments can remain held in the body, later resurfacing as anxiety, defensiveness, or shame.

These reactions aren't flaws; they're signals from the nervous system whispering, *something here still hurts*. When we're activated, the stress response can't always distinguish past from present. The body remembers, even when the mind doesn't. Healing doesn't require reliving the past. It asks for enough safety and support to let what was left unfinished finally move through us.

Whenever something in the present echoes a past wound, the body can react as though the danger has returned. Emotions we couldn't process then rise up now. This overlap between past and present is often called **emotional projection**—when old, unhealed feelings attach to a current situation.

These reactions feel intense not because of what's happening today, but because they originated in a moment that truly was threatening.

In everyday life, this might look like feeling disproportionately upset by a small comment or interpreting neutral feedback as criticism. Instead of getting lost in the reaction, we can meet these moments with curiosity: *What older emotion might this be pointing to?*

We can only recognize, feel, and release past pain when we feel safe enough to do so. Until then, those feelings surface as tension, anxiety, or irritability. For example, a well-meaning coworker offers feedback. I react defensively, feeling instantly small and judged. Later, I notice the familiar echo of childhood criticism. I wasn't responding to my colleague—I was reacting to a memory of not being enough.

Awareness opens a doorway. By naming old pain and meeting it with compassion, we help the body differentiate between then and now. Gradually, the emotional charge softens, and what once felt overwhelming begins to release. In this way, healing happens—not through *force*, but through *allowing*.

Pause to Practice: From identifying with to caring for

Set the intention to welcome emotions as visitors—arriving, staying briefly, and moving on. This practice introduces the spirit of **R.A.I.N.S.** (McDonald, 2021)—**Recognize, Allow, Investigate, Nurture (and non-attachment),** and **Significant Action**. We'll return to it in *Waypoint 4* with more depth; for now, let it simply guide your awareness to support compassion for whatever is present.

Use the prompts below to engage with your emotions as *messengers,* not *definitions* of who you are.

Non-attachment doesn't mean pushing emotions away—it means creating space to observe and respond with compassion, rather than being overwhelmed or defined by them.

For instance, instead of saying, *I'm sad,* try, *I'm noticing sadness in the body, or I'm sitting with sadness right now.* This simple shift reduces the sense of threat and creates room for compassion.

When we have some space between the sensation or emotion, curiosity becomes possible. With space and openness, we might ask: *where does this sadness settle in the body? Does it move, expand, or release when I notice it?*

If you're ready to explore this approach, bring to mind a recent event or conflict that felt stressful. Choose something manageable—nothing overwhelming—but that still lingers in your thoughts or body.

Notice what arises as you recall it, especially the sensations in your body.

On a scale of 1 to 10, how intense do they feel right now? _____

Stay with the sensations, allowing them space to move and speak. You might even imagine breathing space around the feeling with each inhale; this creates more space and capacity to navigate intensity.

Seek understanding by asking questions like, *What do you want me to know?* Or *how old are you?* —especially if the feeling connects to an earlier hurt.

Then, take the role of a compassionate witness. Stay present and curious, offering understanding rather than judgment. Meet this part of yourself as you would a friend in pain, acknowledging,

I see you. I know this is hard. I'm with you.

This is how healing begins: through becoming able to be present, patient, and kind with ourselves.

A kind inner dialogue with ourselves might sound like this:

- **Recognize and Allow**: *I notice tightness in my chest—this is sadness.*
- **Normalize**: *It's okay to feel this. Many people would feel the same.*
- **Nurture**: *I'm here with you. You're safe now.*
- **Release**: Now that this feeling has been seen and supported, it can move through us, instead of getting stuck inside us.

While it can feel awkward at first, this way of relating to ourselves can become quite natural over time.

It helps to practice when we feel calm—having intentional conversations with ourselves creates a pattern we can lean on when life feels overwhelming. Each time we do it, we're investing in a well-worn pathway that gradually shifts from effort to embodiment.

After each practice, pause for a moment and notice how you feel. When we take time to notice even the smallest shifts, it gives us the energy to keep going.

The Body is Our Guest House

As we practice noticing and naming, we begin to experience the body as more than something that simply carries us—it becomes the living interface where all parts of our self can gather. Rather than resisting visitors, we welcome them as important messengers. As we learn to trust them, we can stay present with life as it unfolds. Rūmī's (13th century) teachings—generously translated by our friend Wes Taylor, capture this beautifully—every feeling, even sorrow or fear, arrives with a purpose, clearing space for new growth.

> This body, my friend, is a guesthouse.
> Every morning a new visitor comes running.
> Joy, sorrow, death, or re-birth
> all arrive from the unseen to visit you.
>
> Embrace each and every one, don't let them leave prematurely.
> They, unlike you, do not dwell for eternity.
> Whatever arrives from the unseen world
> is a guest in your heart. Treat it kindly.
>
> When grief comes, sweeping your house clear,
> cleansing, purifying, opening space,
> trust that for every sigh
> a hundred joys will follow in their own time.
>
> Knowing this body is a guesthouse,
> breathe in each new arrival from roof and portal.
>
> Stand as the happiness that lives in your open heart to be a good host.
> Welcome and befriend every one.

Adapted from Masnavi-ye Ma'navi by Jalāl al-Dīn Rūmī (13th century), translated from Persian with AI assistance and interpretive adaptation by Wes Taylor.

This invitation isn't to romanticize pain, but to meet it with reverence. Each emotion, even the ones that unsettle us, contains wisdom about what is asking to be felt, healed, or released. When we meet these inner visitors with curiosity and care, the body becomes a space for reunion rather than resistance.

Pause to Practice: Hosting the Passing Weather

Your body speaks in sensations—tightness, heat, trembling, ache. Pause for a moment and listen. Try approaching the body's signals with curiosity rather than judgment, treating them like visitors with information to offer. If helpful, use the emotional descriptors in **Appendix A** to find language that fits.

- What's my body trying to tell me right now?
- If this feeling had a voice, what would it say?
- What might it need—attention, breath, movement, or rest?

We don't need to fix them; we simply listen—allowing emotion to move rather than constrict, and supporting the nervous system in reading it as information rather than danger.

Notice how it feels when you give a sensation a name. Does it fit, or is there another that resonates more deeply? Stay curious. Each moment of awareness strengthens your capacity to remain grounded during life's inner weather.

Non-attachment and emotional allyship develop gradually. As we attune to the body, emotions shift from feeling dangerous to becoming messengers—bringing insights essential to our wellbeing.

This somatic understanding aligns with both long-standing healing traditions and contemporary scientific perspectives: beneath our thoughts and sensations lies a dynamic field of energy that shapes how we feel and heal. The next section invites us into this terrain by exploring energy medicine as a framework for working with emotion in motion.

Keeping E*motions* in *Motion*

Emotions are energy in motion—literally e-*motion*. When they're suppressed, that flow becomes blocked, creating congestion in both body and mind. Modern science and ancient wisdom converge on this truth: everything is energy, and healing involves restoring its natural movement.

As we come to know how our energy, emotions, and physiology move together, compassion naturally softens what has been held too tightly — creating space to feel and release what no longer serves. Rooted in somatic awareness and energy medicine, these practices help re-pattern the nervous system toward greater balance and resilience.

To bring these ideas into lived experience, the next set of practices translates insight into action—helping energy and emotion return to their natural flow.

Energy Medicine & Somatic Modalities
by Helen Watler, lead somatic energy practitioner

Modern science continues to confirm what wisdom traditions have long understood—that everything is energy, and connection extends beyond what we can see (Oschman, 2000).

Science tells us that 5% of the universe is visible, observable matter. Within this small fraction, the human eye can only perceive matter that emits light within a certain frequency. While birds can perceive magnetic fields and snakes can see in the infrared, we detect only visible light.

We can't see our energy systems, but ancient cultures around the world have mapped them. Chinese Medicine teaches about meridians, while Ayurvedic traditions describe chakras. Indigenous cultures extend this understanding to the land itself, recognizing its energetic presence and honouring a responsibility to care for it—a practice passed down for thousands of years.

When we know about our energy system, we can learn ways to interact with it and help ourselves when life's inevitable challenges show up.

Energy exercises have been developed to help our energy systems repattern, so they remain free flowing, grounded, and balanced. There are simple, easy practices that can help shift our nervous systems from fight/flight/freeze back to rest and digest mode.

The Daily Energy Routine, a practice gifted by Donna Eden, is a tool that helps to support balance, health, and vitality. It takes just a few minutes a day to complete and will be explored further in Week 2 of RTT's CoP program. If you're interested, you can view a video example of the routine by using this QR Code (this is an external link that may change over time).

Another way to bring this understanding into lived experience is through the following practice—**Emotional Freedom Techniques (EFT)**, also known as tapping—which offers a direct way to balance the body's energy while calming the mind.

Pause to Practice: Emotional Freedom Technique/EFT

Emotional Freedom Technique (EFT), also called *tapping*, is a simple mind-body practice used to help regulate stress, emotions, and nervous system responses. It has been applied to everything from chronic pain to PTSD symptoms, anxiety, and to reduce cravings for food and substances.

EFT is Evidence-Based

Dozens of clinical studies have shown that Emotional Freedom Technique (EFT) can reduce symptoms of anxiety, depression, PTSD, and chronic stress. A 2022 review of over 40 clinical trials concluded that EFT meets accepted standards for an evidence-based treatment, with positive effects on both mental and physical health. Reported benefits include lower cortisol levels (the body's main stress hormone), better heart rate variability, and lasting improvements in mood and trauma symptoms (Church et al., 2022). More recently, a 2024 meta-analysis of 18 randomized trials found that EFT significantly reduces depressive symptoms—especially in group settings and among individuals experiencing moderate to severe depression (Seok & Kim, 2024).

When to Use It

You can use EFT when you're feeling anxious, overwhelmed, stuck, or emotionally activated. It's also a helpful practice before or after therapy, medicine sessions, or challenging conversations. You can tap quietly with a few words or speak freely while tapping—whatever helps you stay present and connected with what's coming up.

How to Use It

EFT is a versatile tool that can be practiced independently or with the support of a practitioner.

It involves tapping with your fingertips on specific acupressure points while bringing awareness to difficult thoughts or feelings. Tapping can reduce emotional intensity, calm the body, and create space for new insights or shifts.

Tapping can be practiced in different ways depending on your needs. In one approach, you say a setup phrase such as:

Even though I feel [emotion], I deeply and completely accept myself. Repeat a few reminder words while tapping on a sequence of 8–10 points on the body.

EFT can also be more flexible and expressive. Many people tap while saying what they are honestly feeling in the moment—this could sound like venting, ranting, or naming thoughts that are hard to say out loud (e.g., *This isn't fair, I'm scared they won't understand me, I feel so tired of this,* etc.). Both the structured and expressive forms help the body discharge stress and support emotional release.

Many EFT instructional videos are available online. They explain the basics of EFT and show the tapping points in the figure below, with opportunities to practice along. For participants in the RTT program, you'll learn basic techniques to use EFT on your own and have an opportunity to work with a practitioner in a group setting to practice. **Figure 10** provides a quick reference guide to the EFT tapping points.

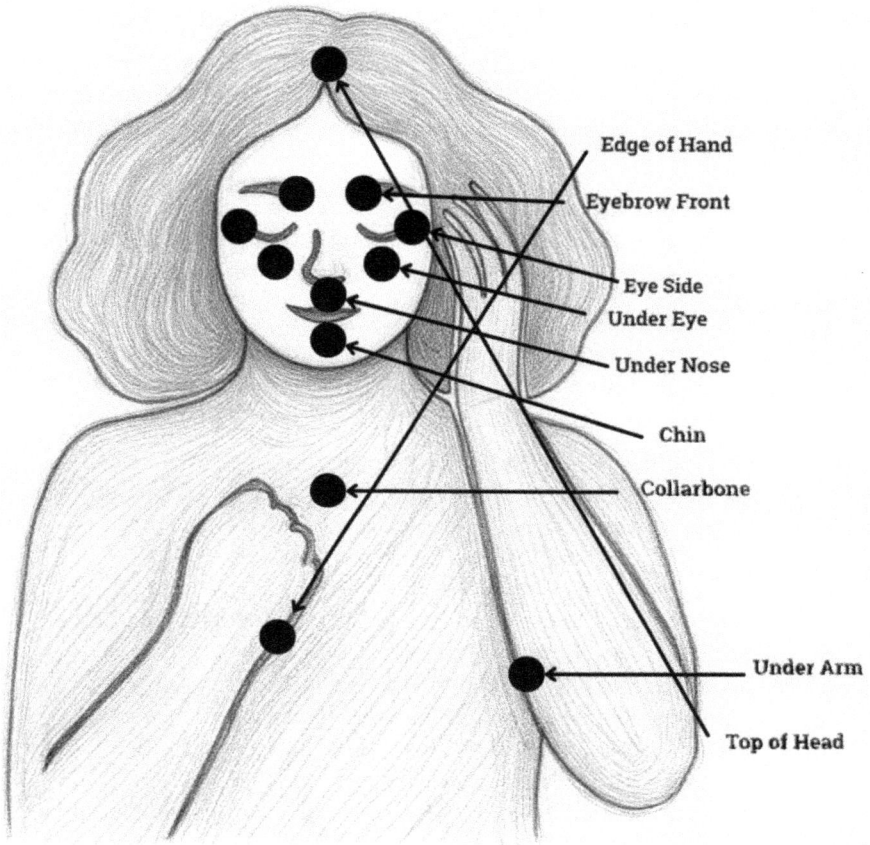

Figure 10. EFT tapping points.

While tapping helps release emotion through movement, writing offers another way—letting energy flow through language and story.

Pause to Practice: Moving stuck energy through writing

Expressive writing helps the body *digest* emotion without overwhelm. Research shows it can ease symptoms of PTSD, anxiety, and depression (Smith et al., 2018), support cognitive function, and promote overall well-being (Tonarelli et al., 2018).

Writing provides both release and integration: it allows emotions to move outward safely, then helps link heart and mind by forming a coherent story about what was felt. Over time, this transforms emotional charge into understanding.

This isn't about perfect sentences—it's about honesty and presence. Let whatever comes—feelings, images, fragments—move onto the page. If your mind drifts, simply bring it back, the way you would in meditation.

Some find this practice natural; others may meet resistance, especially if avoidance has been a common coping style (Sabo Mordechay et al., 2019). If it feels difficult, slow down, breathe, and approach yourself with kindness.

How to Practice

1. **Set aside time:** Choose a quiet space; write for 10–15 minutes.
2. **Check in:** Notice how you feel before beginning.
3. **Write freely:** No censoring, no editing—just expression.
4. **Stay present:** Return to your feelings if distracted.
5. **Keep going:** Let words move, even if disjointed.
6. **Mark the closing:** Pause when you feel complete.
7. **Release:** Optionally burn or shred the pages, symbolizing letting go and inviting renewal.

The goal isn't a finished product—it's integration: allowing emotion to move through and find its rightful place in your story.

In a forest, roots and fungi weave a living network through which trees communicate—receiving nutrients in times of need and giving in times of plenty. This reciprocity sustains the whole ecosystem. In much the same way, we share inner resources through connection. When we're grounded in congruence—true to ourselves—and supported by a sense of coherence—trust in life's meaning and order—we become like well-rooted trees. From that stability, we can both receive nourishment and offer it freely, strengthening the collective resilience that holds us all. The next Waypoint explores this shared ground—the role of community in cultivating resilience.

WAYPOINT 3: SECURING OUR ROOTS IN COMMUNITY

Community isn't a place, a group, or a theory. It's a feeling in the body—a knowing in the heart. —Phillip Dames, RTT Operations Lead

On the pathway to wellness, relationships play a vital role in our capacity for healing and growth. Just as tree roots intertwine beneath the forest floor, our well-being is interdependent. Research affirms this connection: strong social support helps regulate the stress response, easing anxiety and nurturing emotional balance (Acoba, 2024). When we connect and care for each other, our biology reflects that harmony—our nervous systems settle, our capacity to thrive expands.

This waypoint encourages us to return to the wisdom of community—to seek relational spaces that strengthen us through the consistent mirroring of unconditional positive regard and compassionate witnessing. Here, belonging becomes more than a concept; it becomes a felt sense of safety and mutual care.

Community isn't just a group of people—it's a state of connection that lives within us. It's the felt experience of being seen and welcomed as we are, held in unconditional positive regard, and supported by relationships that affirm our belonging, safety, and worth. Research shows that perceived social connection—not merely the number of interactions or memberships—predicts lower mortality, suggesting that how connected we feel is biologically protective (Foster et al., 2023). For this sense of connection to truly take root, mutual intention and trust must be present. Without them, community remains an idea rather than a lived reality.

Drawing from the tree analogy introduced earlier (**Figure 1**), we can see how trees thrive together in a forest. In healthy ecosystems, trees share resources freely, giving and receiving as needed. A tree that requires support isn't seen as a burden—it simply receives what's needed, without shame or hierarchy. Resources flow where they're most required, and when one tree thrives, the whole forest benefits. In the same way, when we cultivate community through mutual care, everyone has a better chance to grow and flourish.

Many of us are shaped by cultures that prioritize self-reliance. We learn to rely only on ourselves and to prove our worth through achievement. We're rewarded for DOing, not for BEing. Competition becomes the norm, and we're told, directly or indirectly, that resources are scarce. This belief in scarcity drives many of us to accumulate, outpace, and perform, even in the presence of abundance. It isolates us. It disconnects us.

In this story, vulnerability is seen as weakness—something to hide rather than share. But this approach contradicts our deep human longing for authenticity, connection, and collaboration. Our biology is wired for togetherness, yet many of us live in patterns of self-protection that create a painful gap between how we're designed to live and how we've learned to survive.

The effects of this disconnection are contagious. Through mirror neurons (described in *Waypoint 1*), our nervous systems continuously attune to the states of those around us, reflecting their cues of safety or threat.

When we're in environments where others are in a survival state, our bodies often follow suit, mirroring that guarded energy. But the opposite is also true. When we're met with trust, openness, and compassion, our mirror neurons reflect that, too. In this way, unconditional positive regard becomes both a metaphor and a mechanism—a literal mirroring of acceptance that helps our nervous systems recalibrate toward safety and connection.

Unconditional positive regard acts as medicine for the nervous system. When we're met with warmth, consistency, and care, we slowly begin to trust—not only others, but ourselves. As we learn to rest in relationships that offer this kind of acceptance, we internalize that tone. Trust allows more of who we are to come forward. We learn to move with care, allowing the body to lead and heal on its own terms.

When met with attunement and safety, vulnerability becomes a bridge—allowing others to meet our wounded selves and helping us reconnect the past with the present.

Vulnerability, in this context, means allowing what's true within us to be seen—our emotions, needs, and stories—without the usual layers of protection. Yet vulnerability alone isn't enough; it needs the right conditions to be healing. When it's met without safety or attunement, it can retraumatize rather than restore. But within trustworthy relationships and environments that can hold what arises, vulnerability becomes transformative. It offers a second chance for the parts of us that once hid for protection to come into the light. Now, supported by greater resources and care, those parts can finally be felt, integrated, and welcomed home. This is *how* we remember our wholeness.

As Elder Geraldine Manson often teaches, "clearing the path between the mind and the heart" reconnects us with our pilot light—the center of our whole, authentic selves. When that pilot light burns bright, its warmth reaches every part of us—even those that learned to stay hidden as a way to survive. In the safety of its glow, as we come to know and trust it, even the most protective parts can find their way back into connection—at their own pace, without force or judgment.

From this lens, thriving then isn't about avoiding challenges but about staying present and steady, even when things are hard. When we lose trust in our ability to navigate life challenges—or when we lack inner or outer safety—our nervous system steps in as protector. In doing so, it can create a barrier between the mind and heart, guarding what feels too tender to face. Yet in genuine relationships, surrounded by the rhythm of community, we can begin to trust again. From this place of safety and belonging, we can regulate, reconnect, and become facilitators of healing—for ourselves and others.

As belonging becomes a lived experience, regulation becomes shared work. Our nervous systems settle more easily in safe company—breaths syncing, voices softening, shoulders lowering. Somatic skills practiced together turn community from an idea into physiology: co-regulation in real time. The practices below are simple but powerful, designed to be used with partners or groups so that safety, rhythm, and presence can circulate like nutrients through a forest.

Co-Regulation and Co-Witnessing: How safety moves between us

Building on the safety and connection that can be found in community, we return to the concept of co-regulation introduced in *Waypoint 1*—how that shared safety and connection show up in our bodies.

Healing becomes possible when we feel safe enough to turn toward emotions that were previously too overwhelming to face. This safety grows through *trustworthy relationships*—those grounded in unconditional positive regard. When we feel seen and accepted, a protective space opens between threat and reaction. Like deep roots stabilizing a tree, this inner steadiness allows us to meet experience with curiosity rather than fear, transforming old patterns of survival into pathways for connection.

Modern neuroscience describes this as parasympathetic regulation; traditional teachings might call it returning to the heart. Both remind us that safety is *felt*, not forced.

Co-regulation is the process of soothing and connecting through relationship with other people and the natural world. These moments of shared safety expand our capacity to hold intense emotions, making it easier to stay present with what was once too much to hold. As this capacity grows, long-buried emotions can surface and integrate.

Mindfulness and somatic awareness practices reinforce this process. They bring us back to the body, steady the breath, and remind the nervous system that it's safe to rest—reducing stress and strengthening resilience (Kabat-Zinn, 2003; O'Connor et al., 2023).

With safety restored in the body and compassion flowing more freely, we become ready to extend that same care outward. Healing deepens when it's witnessed. This capacity to *tune in* to each other prepares us to meet from that same grounded presence.

Returning to the concept of compassionate witnessing introduced in *Waypoint 1*, the next section explores how this awareness becomes a lived practice—shaping the ways we listen and respond.

Compassionate Witnessing: UPR directed outward
by Wes Taylor, Facilitator and Senior Trainer

One powerful way we learn to practice giving unconditional positive regard (UPR) is through cultivating mindful and heartful listening. We can listen at greater depth, using our hearts and bodies to find greater attunement with others. When we attune with others, our nervous systems can relax, strengthening our resilience through a shared sense of connection and presence (reminding us that we are not alone). If we can learn to listen to others in a mindful-heartful way, we can then learn to listen to and treat ourselves with kindness.

A concrete way we practice mindful-heartful listening is through **compassionate witnessing**. Compassionate witnessing is listening for another person's heart and spirit with our bodies and emotions, far more than simply listening with our ears and minds. We are used to listening only with our minds—often preparing something meaningful to say in response, bringing in our similar experience, or advising on the best solutions. These responses usually detract from the self-connection and healing the speaker is needing.

Compassionate witnessing encourages us to use our bodies as a resource to recognize what's alive as we listen, and to sense what's alive in others as they describe their experiences. Being compassionately witnessed offers people the experience of feeling fully seen and heard—and of sensing that their words have touched, moved, or resonated with another, affirming our shared human experience.

Neuroscience helps us understand why this kind of presence is so powerful. When we deeply attune to someone—really feel what they're feeling—our brains activate in similar ways the *mirror neuron* system that was described in *Waypoint 1*. These special brain cells allow us to internally replicate another person's experience, helping us connect through shared emotion and resonance. When someone feels seen and heard at this level, it supports healing not just emotionally, but neurologically (Bonini et al., 2022). *The beautiful part?* This connection is mutual—it calms the nervous system of the one witnessing *and* the one being witnessed.

Confused? That's okay. You will learn better through experiencing it. For those in the RTT CoP program, you'll experience compassionate witnessing by your group facilitators starting in week 1. In week 3, you will receive teaching on how to do it, and then we will encourage you to start in your CoP. It may feel awkward and clunky. That's ok, and to be expected.

There are so many habitual, conditioned patterns in our verbal responses to hearing another person's struggles and pain. Unfortunately, they typically miss the mark. The need to be deeply understood, so important for a healing experience, is stepped over when the responses go in this direction. (Some of these can be useful, but only after deep listening and full presence has been offered.) Here is a list of some of the more common ones:

- Consoling—trying to make the person feel better, reassuring, and encouraging
- Fixing/Advising—offering your ideas about how to solve the challenge
- Sympathizing—focusing on how you're feeling in response to what they have shared, I've been there too, or I can't believe it! I'm so angry for you—that's so unfair…
- Educating—trying to get them to see how they can change their thinking or actions to make things better
- 'One-upping'—telling a story of a worse situation you have endured
- Correcting—showing them how they must have misinterpreted intentions or events
- Interrogating—asking lots of questions to help explore the issue
- Analyzing—explaining to them the dynamics going on in them or in the situation
- Interpreting—diagnosing the issue

All of us will have responded in some, or all of these ways and will continue to do so. We may have even been professionally trained to listen in some of these ways. While some responses have their usefulness in certain situations, we encourage you to turn away from these habitual replies and lean into compassionate witnessing.

When we step away from listening with the typical intent to fix/advise/console/etc., we are inviting our fellow group members into presence as they tune into their own inner pilot light. Our attention on their heart and spirit (instead of the story) can guide their attention to these deeper qualities in themselves and result in greater self-connection. We are also demonstrating that we believe they are capable—they do not require fixing, because they are not broken—there is ample healing intelligence within them. Responding this way is a small but powerful way that we can say *I hold you completely able and whole.*

Responding with compassionate witnessing can be healing for the witnesser—especially for those of us conditioned to "fix." In this practice, we shift from DOing to BEing. Holding space for others strengthens our capacity to offer the same presence to ourselves.

When we realize, we don't have to *DO* anything in these moments, other than to be present and listen with our hearts, our own nervous systems can settle. We don't have to *fix* anyone (again, because none of us is broken, not to mention, we can't fix each other).

To start compassionate witnessing, consider the following (adapted from Rosenberg, 2015; Weingarten, 2003):

- Being fully present (returning your attention to what's happening right now)
- Listening beneath the details of their story for the essential qualities of their internal experience (needs, longings, dreams, what's most important to them)
- Writing down words that resonate (if helpful)
- Recognizing what the feeling is, which may not be articulated or spoken
- Recognizing what the core need or value is, which may not be articulated or spoken
- Reflecting to the speaker the deeper meaning you're hearing from their heart or spirit's longing (e.g., the desire to be truly seen; relief from suffering; mutual respect, etc.)

As you provide compassionate witnessing, you could start something like this:

When I heard you speaking of... (you can use their own words here)
I felt... (physical sensation and emotion)
I sensed that... (value/core need/longing) is important to you

It could sound like this: *John, when you said that you feel as much anger as you do, I noticed tightness in my chest and felt nervous. I got the sense that you just want justice and fairness in this situation—it really matters to you.*

This isn't a formula. Authentic expression of compassion is the main idea. The message, however it sounds, needs focus on these three sentiments:

I see you.
You matter.
I'm with you.

There will be times when you will want so badly to advise, 'cheerlead', or reassure. That's our conditioning. We default to these responses because they make us feel we are DOing something. It's very challenging to sit with the distress of others. It can make us feel helpless, and when we are accustomed to DOing to prove our worth, this can become very painful.

So, when you inadvertently return to the familiar pattern of advising, identifying, or trying to make each other feel better, our facilitators will gently guide you back toward simply **being** a compassionate witness. Let's remember—we are all learning to be skillful, and often, we learn through our unskillful ways.

As with any new practice, awareness grows through experience. Building on these teachings from Wes, the following reflection offers a way to deepen that awareness—moving from fixing to listening with presence and care.

Pause to Practice: From fixing to deep listening

Deep listening is an essential ingredient of compassionate witnessing, and radical presence is what makes deep listening possible. The following are some practical ways to recognize and shift the patterns that can become barriers to presence.

- Listen for the typical responses of fixing, advising, educating, analyzing, etc. in the dialogues you overhear from others in public, or in your novels or TV shows. You will be amazed at how consistent these patterns are in our media and typical social situations. Make it a game—see if you can identify the variety of non-empathic responses using the list above—like a bingo game!
    - See if you can guess at some of the deeper emotions and spiritual longings being expressed by what's being said (e.g. Dorothy in the Wizard of Oz, saying, *"There's no place like home"* is longing for safety, comfort, and familiarity; Chief Brody in Jaws saying, *"You're gonna need a bigger boat!"* is feeling fear and wanting to be safe).
- Recall a time when a family member was upset: Recall your response—did you offer responses that fit the fix-it, correcting, analyzing, or any of the other typical patterns listed above? Which one(s)? What's your best guess at what might have been the deeper emotions and spiritual longings they were communicating? See if you can craft a verbal response, including those guesses that you could imagine offering.

As our capacity to witness one another with compassion grows, we naturally begin to extend that same presence inward. This marks the next layer of practice—listening to the many parts of ourselves: the tender parts, the protective parts, the wounded parts, and the ones that have quietly carried us for years. Each is worthy of the unconditional regard we so readily offer others. The following Waypoint, on *inner healing intelligence*, helps us lean more deeply into this inward turning—trusting the innate wisdom within each part, a wisdom that knows how to heal when given space and the right conditions.

WAYPOINT 4: INNER HEALING INTELLIGENCE & R.A.I.N.

Healing isn't something we have to earn—it's an innate intelligence we all carry. Like a seed, it waits for the right conditions to grow. These conditions are often created through safe, supportive relationships, where compassion and presence help awaken our **inner healing intelligence**. When we feel ready, and with the right support, we can begin to turn inward with care. Healing doesn't come from pushing—it comes from trusting the body's wisdom and allowing safety and connection to lead the way.

Inner Healing Intelligence: The whisper of inner knowing

The idea of inner healing intelligence has been described as an internal compass that, under the right conditions, knows how to guide us toward transformation (Grof & Grof, 2010). A wound heals spontaneously—no thought required. Likewise, the psyche carries an innate capacity for spontaneous healing. We access this potential by intentionally stepping out of thought. In this state of thoughtlessness, we tap into the wisdom and intuition of the gut and heart brain. From here, we can loosen habitual cravings and cultivate discernment, allowing right action to emerge with greater ease.

Arriving here is never a permanent destination or a fixed outcome. The mind will inevitably hijack our best efforts. It's a practice of noticing and returning to our somatic intelligence—our *elder in residence*—when navigating the inevitable bumps along the way.

It's this internal intelligence that determines what surfaces and when, bringing forward what's ready to heal at each stage (Grof, 2013). As we come to trust our internal wisdom, we start to cooperate with the change process rather than overthinking it or trying to force it. We learn to move at the body's speed—especially when the mind stomps its feet in impatience, as it tends to do.

Just as a plant requires the right conditions to grow, our healing potential depends on context. A supportive environment—both internal and external—provides the fertile ground needed for this intelligence to thrive. When people feel safe, seen, and connected, their innate capacity for balance and well-being naturally emerges (McEwen, 1998; Porges, 2022).

A Slow and Steady Approach

It's important to remember that not everyone can access this capacity easily. For those living with unresolved trauma, chronic stress, or systemic oppression, the nervous system may be creating too much noise to hear the signal of the inner healer. This doesn't mean the intelligence is absent—it means the body is still doing its job: protecting us (van der Kolk, 2014; Porges, 2011).

Moving at the pace of trust means honouring the rhythm of our most protective parts. For some, this process will unfold slowly—and that's okay. Healing isn't a race; it's a relationship.

Compassion is key, allowing us to honour each part's pace with unconditional positive regard. When we meet our protectors with patience rather than pressure, they begin to soften. Safety expands, and the inner healing intelligence—the organizing wisdom within—can move more freely (Ogden & Fisher, 2015).

Creating the Conditions for Healing

Healing starts with a pause—a breath that clears the noise and lets us hear the truth beneath the chatter. Practices that incorporate breath, movement, touch, and connection can help settle internal noise, allowing the quiet voice of our inner healer to be heard. In this way, healing doesn't happen by pushing—it happens when we become safe and secure enough to soften and unfold like a grip that's been holding on too long.

Throughout this curriculum, many tools support the nervous system to build capacity for this listening. *Unconditional positive regard* is the primary medicine and *Communities of Practice* are the living soil that expand our window of tolerance—creating the fertile ground where the whisper of inner wisdom can take root, allowing the medicine to be absorbed, integrated, and embodied.

While many people find relief through relational support, breathwork, and somatic practices, there are times when the nervous system is so activated that these tools alone may not suffice. In such cases, additional supports—such as pharmaceutical or psychedelic medicines—can assist with creating space for healing to occur. To understand how these medicines support healing, we explore the nature of non-ordinary states of consciousness in **Appendix B**. These are not cures, nor are they necessary for everyone. But when they are used thoughtfully and in alignment with each person's needs, they can act like gardening tools—loosening the soil, supporting regulation, and widening the window of tolerance so that insights can extend their roots deep enough to break through hard ground and become embodied. Like all tools in the healing process, they are most effective when integrated with practices that nurture safety, connection, and self-awareness.

Many body-based practices can also help settle the nervous system and create the conditions for our inner compass to guide us toward growth:

- Breathwork (e.g., 4–7–8 breathing, cyclic sighing)
- Gentle movement (e.g., yoga, tai chi, walking)
- Comforting touch (e.g., hand on heart, butterfly hug)
- Meditation or mindful awareness
- Naming of emotions as they arise (e.g., I notice tightness in my chest)
- Expressive writing to release tension
- Compassionate witnessing with a trusted other
- Buddy check-ins to share sensations and emotions
- Therapeutic co-regulation through attuned presence
- Connecting with nature
- Sensory anchoring (noticing sounds, textures, smells)

These practices aren't about doing more—they're invitations to listen, soften, and remember what's already whole within.

To access our inner healing intelligence, we learn to turn inward—beyond the noise of self-criticism or distraction. Practices such as **R.A.I.N.**, introduced in *Waypoint 2*, offer structured ways to reconnect with this wisdom and restore the natural flow of healing from within.

Michele McDonald (n.d.) first developed the RAIN practice, and Tara Brach (2019) later adapted it by changing the last step from non-identifying to nurturing. In RTT, we build on their work by adding both nurturing and *non-attachment*, along with *significant actions* to strengthen agency and integration. These steps invite us to meet each moment with presence, acceptance, curiosity, compassion, and choice—creating

Recognize
Notice what you are

Allow
Let your thoughts and emotions be

Investigate
Be kind to yourself

Nurture
Treat yourself like a dear other

an inner space where inner healing intelligence can lead the way.

Drawing on the teachings of Julia Sheffield, a senior facilitator in RTT, we often discover that we meet our emotions with the *opposite* of the RAIN practice. McDonald calls this **DROP**—representing *Distraction, Resistance, Oblivious,* or *Personalizing.* When these patterns arise, awareness becomes a turning point. With even a small pause, we can soften the grip of reactivity and meet what's here with a gentler presence.

Distracted
Mind all over the place

Resistant
Tensing up against

Oblivious
Blind to what's real

Taking it Personally
Inwardly holding pain

Awareness gives us choice—an intention that shapes the next breath, the next gesture, the next step. Each moment asks us quietly: *Will we move toward entanglement or toward freedom?*

Now that we have a few tools that help us turn inward, let's take a moment to explore the landscape.

Pause to Reflect: How's your relationship with your inner healer?

Consider the life of a seed maturing into a plant.

Growth doesn't happen all at once—it unfolds gradually, shaped by the conditions around and within us. Just as a seed depends on soil, sunlight, and water, your inner healer thrives in an environment of care, intention, and trust.

The following questions help us explore our relationship with our innate healing intelligence—the internal compass that supports our growth and guides us toward what we need most.

- What daily practices or habits could help you cultivate this inner garden—the conditions in which growth can take root?
- What relationships, boundaries, or rituals nourish the soil of your well-being and allow new life to flourish?
- What patterns or obligations might need care-full pruning, making space for light and new energy to reach what's ready to grow?
- What's one small but *significant action* you can commit to—something that honours your innate healing intelligence and helps it take root and flourish?

Seed your intention. Jot it down.

Let it be a seed of intention—planted today, tended with care, and pruned as needed so it can grow strong in its own season.

As you hold this intention, notice how it feels in your body. Every seed of change begins in awareness, then takes form through practice. Now, we'll turn inward—to listen, to breathe, and to follow the wisdom that already lives within you.

Pause to Practice: Following wisdom

Visualize a challenging situation in your life, such as an argument with a close friend. Connect with your inner healer by following your breath, allowing it to breathe space around any sensations and emotions that arise.

From this place, ask yourself:

- What really matters to me in this situation?
- How can I respond in a way that aligns with my well-being and values?
- Who is showing up right now? Is it a younger or protective part of me that needs care, or the wise, healing part that can listen with compassion?

As introduced in *Waypoint 2*, when we experience pain in a past relationship, that same pain or sense of threat can project onto present-day events. This happens because our inner healing intelligence is always trying to resolve areas of stickiness—where past emotions remain lodged in the body. By recognizing when a younger or protective part is surfacing, we can meet that part with curiosity rather than judgment.

If we're aware of this connection, we're better positioned to turn toward the emotion and see the opportunity to heal a past wound in the present moment. If you find yourself over-identifying with the emotion, try naming the part of you that's coming forward. This can help distinguish the anxious or protective part from the inner healing intelligence that's trying to emerge. This practice empowers you to confront challenges with clarity and authenticity, allowing you to make deliberate choices instead of impulsive reactions.

Let's put this into action:

Think back to the last time your nervous system was activated—perhaps leading to a reaction you're not proud of.

- What questions could you have asked your inner healer in that moment?
- What parts of yourself surfaced during that experience?
- What words could you offer those parts to let them know they've been heard and that you'll take care of them?

This practice strengthens our connection to the part of us that already knows how to heal—and helps us meet *every* part with compassion.

Integrating R.A.I.N.S. into Daily Life

Trauma isn't defined by what happened to us, but by how safe we feel to be with the emotions swirling inside. Healing begins when we have the space and support to notice and nurture our inner experiences, and the confidence to take a meaningful step forward when the time is right.

The R.A.I.N.S. technique—**R**ecognize, **A**llow, **I**nvestigate, **N**urture, and **S**ignificant Action— is a practice we often return to throughout the program. It offers a fresh framework for meeting the body with curiosity and compassion, helping you notice your thoughts and emotions without judgment. By taking these steps, we strengthen congruence between what we feel and how we live.

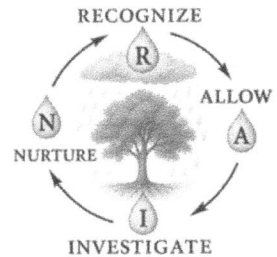

At first, this inner work can feel awkward—perhaps even a little cringy—especially if we're not used to paying attention to what's happening inside. It can feel like trying to reconnect with someone you've been distant from for a long time. But with time, patience, and self-compassion, that relationship with *our selves*—the many parts of self—begins to soften. The sensations, emotions, and patterns we once avoided start to feel like familiar messengers, not threats.

The final step is *significant action* (elaborated in *Waypoint 7*)—is crucial, reminding us that insight alone remains theoretical rather than embodied, where *BEing informs DOing*. Small, value-aligned actions translate awareness into lived experience and sustained change. It's not about pushing or rushing to fix—it's about moving intentionally, aligning what we do with what truly matters. This step builds agency—the felt sense that we can meet life as active participants rather than passive recipients. It's like climbing onto a surfboard in the face of a towering wave: uncertain, perhaps effortful, yet profoundly empowering. Each act of choosing—even the smallest one—reminds us that we are not powerless. We can ride the wave instead of being pulled under by it.

Grounding practices like R.A.I.N.S help calm the nervous system by creating a sense of safety. This not only settles us but also builds resilience—key insights from seminal psychologist Stephen Porges' work on how safety shapes regulation (2011).

The following reflection provides a practical approach to engaging with R.A.I.N.S. in real-time, particularly during moments of overwhelm or overstimulation.

Pause to Reflect: Bringing R.A.I.N.S. to life

Imagine being in a highly stimulating environment—children playing, phones ringing, call bells chiming—and beginning to feel overwhelmed. In these moments, turning to the R.A.I.N.S. process can restore steadiness and choice.

Recognize what's happening—both around and within you. Notice the external challenge and acknowledge what may be beyond your direct control. Then turn inward: *What sensations are present? Is your body safe in this moment?* Visualize the experience as weather passing through. You're not the storm; you're the observer.

Allow emotions to rise without resistance. Let them be what they are, without trying to fix or suppress them. Sometimes, the most courageous act is to stay with what's uncomfortable, trusting that like the weather, it will pass. Take a slow breath and permit yourself simply to feel.

Investigate with curiosity. *What's this feeling trying to tell you?* Notice patterns, stories, or urges to react. Ask: *What am I believing right now? What might this emotion need?* Bringing awareness here invites the wise, observing self back online.

Nurture what arises. Try speaking to yourself as you would someone you hold dear: *It's okay to feel this.* Offer reassurance to your nervous system—place a hand over your heart or take a slow exhale. These gestures signal safety and connection, softening the body's instinct to fight or flee.

Non-Attachment: Surrender the outcome.
Ask yourself: *Do I truly control this outcome, or only how I meet it?*
Letting go of control doesn't mean giving up or disengaging—it means releasing the grasp on how things *must* turn out. When our grip softens, space opens for discernment and compassionate action. As we step back from the heat of reactivity—like leaning away from a flame—we can see more clearly and respond from steadiness rather than fear.

From that place of steadiness, choose a **significant action**—or a deliberate pause—that supports resolution, reframing, or reconnection. Sometimes this means taking a break, having an honest conversation, or simply breathing before responding. Each intentional act is a bridge between awareness and change.

Example 1 – Workplace Stress

A busy shift builds tension in my shoulders; my breath shortens.

- **Recognize:** My body feels tight and overwhelmed.
- **Allow:** I pause for one full breath, letting the tension be there.
- **Investigate:** *What does my body need right now?* I notice I haven't eaten or taken a break.
- **Nurture:** It's okay—I'm doing my best. My body needs care right now.
  - o **Non-Attachment:** I'm learning to loosen my grip on doing everything perfectly.
- **Significant Action:** I plan a short break and let my team know.

Example 2 – Difficult Conversation

Before a challenging talk with a friend, I feel a knot in my stomach.

- **Recognize:** My body feels anxious about being misunderstood.
- **Allow:** I take a breath, letting the fear be there without judgment.
- **Investigate:** *What's underneath this?* I sense a fear of losing connection.
- **Nurture:** It's okay to care this much. You can speak honestly and kindly.
  - o **Non-Attachment:** I can't control how the other person responds—but I can stay present and true to my intention.
- **Significant Action:** I start the conversation, speaking honestly with my friend about my fears of losing them.

Sensations are not problems—they're pathways back to connection. Each time we turn toward our experience rather than away from it, we strengthen our ability to stay present and respond with compassion. Over time, this steady tending of awareness becomes the soil where resilience and wisdom take root—allowing our healing intelligence to blossom in its own season.

Reflect: Take a moment to recall a recent challenging situation. After moving through the first four steps of R.A.I.N.S., *what significant action—or non-action— was being called for at that moment?*

As we learn to act from this grounded awareness, we also discover the importance of what comes after action—the *sacred pause*. Growth often happens not in the doing, but in the in-between. In the next Waypoint, we explore liminal space—the threshold between what was and what's becoming—where transformation unfolds.

WAYPOINT 5: LIMINAL SPACE & THE WINDOW OF TOLERANCE

Between the unravelling of what was and the forming of what will be, we meet the sacred uncertainty of becoming.

Crossing Thresholds

Each threshold we cross—whether emotional, relational, or spiritual—marks a liminal space: a pause between what was and what's next. Liminal comes from the Latin limen, meaning threshold. As contemplative teacher, Richard Rohr (1999) observes, this in-between space is where transformation becomes possible. These moments invite us to meet the unknown with curiosity rather than fear.

Life can feel like a snow globe—everything stirred and unclear. In time, the flurries settle, and what matters comes back into view. This image captures the essence of liminal space. During transitions, it can feel as though everything familiar has been shaken loose. The clarity we once relied on may be obscured, and the path ahead uncertain. But, like the snow globe, if we pause and allow the swirling to settle, a new landscape begins to emerge.

Emotional disorientation is not only normal but also essential to transformation. Liminal space is often marked by confusion, doubt, and emotional turbulence—conditions that, when held with awareness, allow new perspectives to emerge (Irving et al., 2019). As we expand our window of tolerance, we grow our capacity to experience discomfort without becoming overwhelmed. In this balanced space between activation and calm, integration and healing become possible.

Before we move into practices for navigating these edges, let's pause. Thresholds often appear quietly—in moments of pause, transition, uncertainty, or stillness—inviting us to notice what's shifting within and around us.

Pause to Reflect: Recognizing liminal spaces

Notice when you find yourself in a threshold moment. These may arise during transitions, conversations, or pauses in daily life. *What sensations, thoughts, or emotions signal that you're standing at the edge between your old ways of being and something new?*

Thresholds can feel both unsettling and sacred. When we can recognize that we are in a liminal space—neither here nor there—we can choose presence over reactivity, curiosity over control.

Reflections on Liminal Space

by Margaret Huml, a nurse and fellow RTT traveller

> I've crossed a threshold into a space between—no longer who I was, not yet who I'm becoming. It's uncomfortable, slow, and unknown. Sometimes I want to go back, but I can't. I sit, breathe, and notice.
>
> In this waiting space, my mind urges action, decisions, movement. But my heart whispers, *just be.*
>
> Healing isn't a timeline—it's a process. So, I sit, breathe, pause, and return to my *BEing* when I can.
>
> I wander in nature, seeking anchors—in community, in unconditional positive regard. Even when I feel messy or weary, I show up. There's beauty in the waiting, even when it's excruciating.
>
> Expansion feels like success, but contraction holds depth. *Can I meet myself in discomfort?* I try—with compassion, gentleness, and love.
>
> This space is sacred. It invites me to listen, to tend, to befriend what arises. I am not lost—I am found. Connected to source, to community, to my Being.
>
> Healing ripples outward. As I walk this path, I remember: a life lived in healing is a life well lived.

This poem beautifully captures the essence of liminality—the sacred in-between where transformation unfolds. From this place of stillness and awareness, we can begin to explore how to care for ourselves when the intensity of transformation feels like too much.

At the Edge of Overwhelm: A simple guide

Move with care. When we try to grow too quickly, it can backfire—leading to overwhelm and slowing us down in the long run. Pacing ourselves helps us stay grounded; when the process moves too fast, it can trigger shutdown or disconnection, slowing our growth and healing capacity (Corrigan et al., 2010). Taking things one step at a time makes it easier to stay with the process and let change take root.

When we're in a **liminal space**—a time of transition, uncertainty, or emotional intensity—it's easy to feel lost, scattered, or overwhelmed. Our nervous system may shift into fight, flight, freeze, or collapse as it struggles to make sense of what feels unpredictable or unsafe. Neuroscience shows that in these moments, **structure and predictability act as medicine**—creating a steady rhythm the body can lean into, calming stress responses, and helping us return to a felt sense of steadiness and safety.

58

Step 1: Create Predictable Anchors

Introduce simple routines that bring a sense of order. They don't need to be rigid—just consistent enough to offer stability. Examples:

- Morning meditation or breathwork
- A short walk or movement practice
- Journaling or reading something grounding
- Preparing nourishing food at regular times

These anchors help your system feel safe and oriented.

Step 2: Choose One Thing at a Time

When everything feels chaotic, simplify. Ask: *What's one small thing I can do right now to support myself?* Even brushing your teeth, making tea, or stepping outside can be a meaningful act of regulation.

Step 3: Use Familiar Tools

Return to practices that have helped you before. This might include:

- Tapping (EFT)
- 4-7-8 breathing
- Placing a hand on your heart or belly
- Listening to calming music or nature sounds

The goal isn't to fix or escape the discomfort—but to **stay connected to yourself** within it.

Step 4: Be Gentle

You don't need to be perfect. You don't need to feel better right away. Just notice: *Can I meet myself here with kindness?* Gentleness is the path back to your window of tolerance.

These are the thresholds when something shifts—a limiting belief, a worn-out pattern, or energy that's been stuck for years. These moments don't usually come with clarity right away, but they pave the way for healing and growth.

Though the liminal space may feel uneasy, it's also rich with potential. It asks us to slow down, trust the process, and remain curious. This in-between isn't a detour; it's part of the path, an essential part of the journey where transformation begins.

As shown in **Figure 11**, understanding our *window of tolerance* makes it easier to navigate liminal spaces. This concept helps us manage discomfort and appreciate these transitional periods, turning them into opportunities for growth rather than something to fear.

Our ability to stay grounded amid stress—what we call the window of tolerance—is shaped by our life experiences and nervous system. When we're within this window, we feel capable and connected. When we're outside it, things can feel overwhelming or numb. Daniel Siegel (1999) introduced this concept to help us understand how the nervous system responds to challenge and why safety and regulation are essential for healing.

Think of **hyperarousal** as a car speeding too fast. Linked to the fight-or-flight response, it might show up as trouble focusing, irritability, anger, panic, anxiety, or self-destructive behaviors. On the other side, **hypoarousal** is like the car stalling—connected to the freeze response and often experienced as exhaustion, depression, numbness, or disconnection (dissociation). People often move between these states, and trauma or extreme stress can make these shifts more likely.

Each person's window of tolerance is unique. It's shaped by many factors—our biology, early experiences, support systems, coping tools, and the environments we live and work in. A wider window means we can experience strong emotions or challenges without tipping into overwhelm. A narrower window means our body is more likely to interpret circumstances as threatening rather than manageable. When this happens, we might avoid new situations or people to stay within our comfort zone.

But when we keep limiting ourselves, our capacity to cope can shrink over time. As we learn to expand our window—through awareness, support, and practice—we build the ability to face life's ups and downs with more confidence and **equanimity**—a steady, balanced state of mind that helps us stay grounded, even when things feel uncertain.

Figure 11. can handle challenges with stability. A narrowed window makes us more likely to shift into hyperarousal (anxious, overwhelmed) or hypoarousal (numb, shut down).

When we're approaching or beyond our window of tolerance, the next step is to invite the body back into safety. The body holds both the memory of distress and the wisdom to restore balance. Soothing through breath, touch, or grounding helps us return to the present moment, reminding the nervous system that it's safe enough to soften.

Bridging Awareness and Embodiment

Recognizing overwhelm is the first step, but awareness alone doesn't create regulation. We may understand what's happening long before we feel any change in the body. In this space between knowing and feeling, frustration or shame can surface—but it's also where healing begins.

In these moments, the nervous system learns a new rhythm, and the mind and body start to rebuild trust. We access patience by remembering that healing isn't about forcing calm—it's about creating the conditions for safety to return.

We bridge awareness and embodiment by soothing the body through breath, touch, and presence. Each time we do, we remind the body that it's safe to soften and receive. With practice, these experiences build on each other, and regulation becomes something we feel—not just something we understand.

Soothing the Body

When life feels overwhelming, our instinct may be to pull away, shut down, or rush through discomfort—yet soothing encourages us to slow down and stay present in these in-between moments. It's the practice of helping the body feel calm, supported, and nurtured. Trauma often occurs when something painful happens without a sense of safety or connection. By learning how to soothe ourselves—and allowing others to soothe us—we begin to repair those ruptures. Each act of soothing teaches the nervous system that safety can return, even after stress or pain.

Soothing involves simple actions that remind the body it's safe now. When our nervous system receives that message, our muscles release, our breathing steadies, and our emotions become easier to hold with kindness.

Everyone's way of soothing is different. Some people find calm through slow, deep breathing, gentle movement, or meditation. Others connect through music, journaling, time in nature, vigorous exercise, cold water immersion, or talking with someone who feels safe. You might also find comfort in sensory experiences—like warmth, touch, scent, or rhythm.

The ability to soothe ourselves when we feel unsteady is a core part of emotional well-being. It helps us feel more grounded in liminal spaces, offering a sense of stability as we move through change. Soothing doesn't make uncertainty disappear—it helps us rest within it, knowing that we can meet whatever arises with compassion and care.

The body learns safety through sensation. Soothing begins with the breath and deepens with touch, reminding our nervous systems that they are safe and supported.

Pause to Practice: Soothing with breath

Breath is a powerful way to calm the nervous system. A recent study found cyclic sighing to be the most effective breathwork method—compared to box breathing, cyclic hyperventilation, and meditation—for reducing physiological activation and improving emotional well-being (Balban et al., 2023).

Cyclic sighing involves:

A deep breath in
A second shorter inhale until your lungs are full
A long, slow exhale until all the air is gone

Practicing this for just a few minutes a day can calm the body and steady the mind. Once we're familiar with breath as a physiological anchor, we can also experience it as a bridge into awareness itself.

Breath as a Bridge to Presence
by Dr. Crosbie Watler, lead psychiatrist

Presence could be defined as bringing *still awareness* to whatever is arising, right here, right now. It's experiencing this moment, free of any judgment or clutter from the mind field. Two truths help cultivate presence, building our capacity to use our attention with intention:

Attention is finite; metaphorically, we have $100 of attention, and we should reflect on whether we are investing our attention wisely. *Are my thoughts serving any purpose or simply cluttering space, creating suffering?* The acronym W.A.I.T. is a great reminder: *Why Am I Thinking? Is it serving any purpose?* At these times, we are called to step out of thought and into presence, awareness without thought.

Attention is like fertilizer. Attention can only be in one place at a time. When we believe that we are multitasking, in truth, our attention shifts back and forth. What we attend to grows. Research supports this notion, showing that where we place our attention reshapes how we perceive, feel, and act. It does so by filtering out distractions and amplifying what matters (van Ede et al., 2025). Like a discerning gardener, we are called to notice whether we're feeding the veggies or the weeds. Without this awareness, the mind takes over, repeating old patterns that don't serve us—or the people around us.

When we lose presence to the stickiness of the mind, our bodies remind us that we've lost it. Presence has been usurped by thought addiction—a challenge we all share, but one we can manage by noticing what's arising in the body. *What do you feel in the body—anxious, afraid, sad, or angry?* Whatever the distressing emotion, it lands as a felt sense in the body. This link can serve as a reminder to step out of thought, coming to know and trust the wisdom and intuition that live in the space between our thoughts.

Our reliable and omnipresent ally is awareness of breath and the space it creates in the body. We shift our attention with intention, bringing our awareness from above the neck (mind field) to below the neck (the body). Following our breath in and down, pause, then up and out, with 100% of our attention on the flow of breath and the space it creates in the body. This practice builds on the two points above—if our attention is fully grounded in awareness of breath, there is simply no attention or bandwidth left for the turning mind.

Imagine a light switch on your sternum, your breastbone: *is my attention above the neck, or below the neck?* Use the mind to think when it's of service to you, notice (in the body) when it isn't. When our thoughts create stress, we can simply step out of them—no need to judge or resist. Light switch down as we shift awareness to the breath and inner space. What you experience in that still space between your thoughts is your true nature, free of the stickiness of ego and attachment. Pilot light, true nature, being self, consciousness, all are attempts to describe something that can't be named but rather is *felt*. Whatever you experience there is your truth, your inner divinity.

Breath awareness anchors our awareness in the present moment, aligning us with what is, instead of what we wish it to be. It's a resource that's always available. Practice these two breathing techniques, noticing how settled you feel, before and after.

- **4-2-4 breath:** Inhale for 4, pause for 2, exhale for 4—no need to count precisely, just approximately. Before speaking, pause briefly after the inhale to connect with your inner space, allowing words to arise from presence. This mirrors yogic principles of aligning breath with inner wisdom/healing intelligence before action. This breath is a versatile ally, as we can practice it when in DOing mode—conversations, activities.
- **4-7-8 breath:** Inhale for 4, pause for 7, exhale for 8.

Experiment with both, as they have a different feel and different applications.

Consider the 4-2-4 breath as the foundation for heartfelt conversations and the 4-7-8 breath for settling activation when there is the luxury of nothing to do.

We have thousands of waking breaths per day, and each is an opportunity to build a relationship with the wisdom and well-being that greets us in the space between our thoughts. Don't wait for a crisis, rather, maintain an ongoing curiosity: *How grounded am I?* Build the connection, the relationship with presence, notice when you lose it, as we will, and simply return to it.

Set an intention this week to try speaking from the pause between breaths. Listen from there as well. I've been told that it's not the notes in music that draw the listener in, it's the space between the notes.

In early Buddhist teachings, mindfulness of breathing was not solely about focused attention, but about cultivating spacious awareness—including the natural rhythm and pauses between breaths, which serve as gateways to presence and insight (Anālayo, 2019).

Breath practices help prepare us for deeper inner work by calming the nervous system, reducing reactivity, and bringing our attention back into the body. When we're more settled and present, we can meet challenging emotions, thoughts, and patterns with greater clarity and steadiness.

From this grounded place, revisit R.A.I.N.(N) with particular attention to the second N—nurture and non-attachment. This is the art of leaning back into what is, rather than grasping for what we wish it were. In this spaciousness, clarity, discernment, and wise action have room to emerge. Without the stickiness of attachment, we respond with greater ease, compassion, and perspective.

Soothing with Touch: Somatic resourcing

When we feel physical pain, our instinct is to soothe it—often by holding or gently rubbing the area. In the same way, intentional touch can help ease emotional pain. This kind of touch, called affective touch, activates special nerve fibres that send signals of safety and comfort to the brain. These signals support emotional regulation, reduce stress, and nurture well-being throughout life (Kidd et al., 2023).

Touch can also soften emotional distress in the moment, calming the body's stress response and helping us recover after difficult experiences (Della Longa et al., 2025). It even stimulates the release of oxytocin—a hormone that lowers stress, boosts immunity, and fosters healing and social connection (Uvnäs-Moberg & Petersson, 2022).

When used in ways that feel safe and comforting, touch can settle the body and quiet the mind. It reminds us: we're here, we're safe, we're held. Simple gestures—like wrapping your arms around yourself in a self-hug or imagining a protective bubble—can help you feel grounded when emotions run high, or the world feels overwhelming. These small acts create a sense of boundary, calm, and reassurance for your nervous system.

WAYPOINT 6: EMOTIONAL CONDITIONING

Riding the 90-second wave. When an emotion arises, the body releases a chemical wave that lasts ~ 90 seconds. After that, it's our thoughts keeping it going (Taylor, 2008).

Emotions aren't problems to fix—they're messengers, pointing us toward what needs care and attention. In this Waypoint, we shift from resisting emotions to respecting them. Instead of suppressing or getting swept away, we learn to listen with curiosity and compassion.

This is **emotional conditioning**: calming the nervous system, attuning to our natural rhythm, and responding from our inner signal rather than old wounds or outside pressure. Over time, we begin to trust the deeper intelligence within us—a wisdom that knows how to restore balance when we give it space. Emotions become allies, offering insight, connection, and a way back to our true nature.

Emotional regulation is like finding your stance on a surfboard—it gives you stability so you don't get thrown off by the first big wave. It's what allows you to pause, breathe, and choose your next move instead of reacting on autopilot. **Emotional rhythm**, on the other hand, is about trusting the ocean itself—the natural rise and fall of feelings that come and go like waves. When we fight the wave, we exhaust ourselves. When we trust its intelligence, we learn to move with it.

Regulation creates the space for rhythm to emerge. Without it, the nervous system often steps in as a protector, shutting down expression to keep us safe. But when we tune into our inner *signal*—the steady pilot light beneath the *noise*—we can hold space for the intensity of the wave without losing our balance. Over time, emotions stop feeling like something to control and start feeling like something to harmonize with. Our rhythm begins to align with that deeper intelligence—guided by values, purpose, and meaning—so we're not just surviving, we're surfing life with coherence.

The more we trust and align with that signal, the less threatening external noise becomes. From this place of inner strength, we can meet the noise with compassion—treating it as a dear *other* rather than something to fight or suppress. Emotions can then be felt, witnessed, and released. Even if we can't eliminate the noise, we can learn to turn the volume down. Research supports this approach. When we activate and align with our core values—even in the midst of external stress—we strengthen our sense of coherence and overall well-being (Russo-Netzer & Atad, 2024).

Noise is often tied to unresolved emotions related to past events, projected onto present-day experiences and relationships—or from emotional transference, when we absorb others' feelings as if they were our own. Sometimes, what we're feeling doesn't belong to us.

A lighthearted Polish proverb, often shared by RTT senior facilitator Julia Sheffield, speaks to this truth: the importance of compassionate differentiation—staying grounded in our own signal while recognizing that not every emotional frequency we pick up belongs to us:

Not my circus. Not my monkeys.

We already have enough to tend in our own "circus"—and plenty of monkeys on our backs—without taking on what belongs to others. This isn't just metaphorical; research shows that when someone around us is anxious, sad, or joyful, the same parts of our brain that process those emotions can light up too (Fu et al., 2025). While this mirroring helps us empathize, it can also blur the boundaries between our feelings and theirs—making it harder to know where their experience ends and ours begins.

With practice, we can become more aware of when we're caught up in another's circus. When that happens, a gentle cue can help: *Not me, not mine— return to sender, with compassion.*

This is where emotional differentiation becomes essential. When we live from the tenderness beneath our defenses, we become steady lamps of compassion—able to illuminate the way for ourselves and others without losing our center.

Differentiating Signal from Noise

It used to be noise,
but now it is a signal
and I love the sound.
—*Megan McLaren, MCC, RCC, a therapist and fellow RTT traveller*

Think back to the days of analogue radios. As we turned the dial, static filled the space between stations. That static was **noise**, obscuring the **signal** of the station we wanted to hear. Similarly, our mental chatter—shaped by cultural conditioning and external opinions—can drown out the signal of our inherently worthy essence. **Figure 12** illustrates this relationship: the signal of who we are at our core versus the passing noise within and around us.

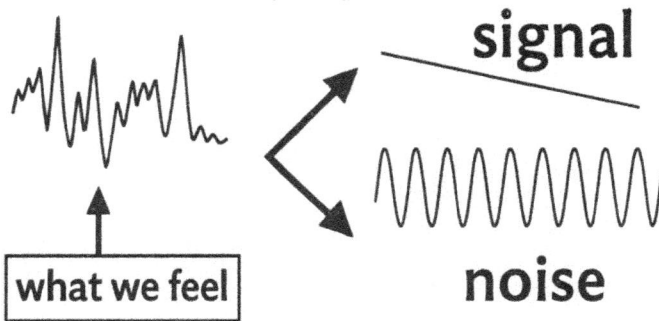

Figure 12. Our true nature is like a clear signal beneath the noise. While emotions and thoughts swirl around us, tuning into the steady signal helps us reconnect with true nature.

66

When noise overwhelms us—through anxious thoughts about climate change or life's uncertainties—it can distort our sense of self. Crystal, a senior clinician on the RTT team, describes this early effort to tune into true nature a bit like *trying to hear a whisper inside a scream.* As we build a relationship with that deeper part of ourselves, the whispers become easier to recognize. The breath can be a helpful ally in this process, calming the body and creating space for us to hear the subtle. The following practice is a good choice to support calming and clearing.

Pause to Practice: Settling the body with the 4-7-8 breath

The 4-7-8 breath is a simple and effective way to calm both body and mind. Slow, paced breathing activates the parasympathetic nervous system—your body's natural relaxation response—helping to slow heart rate, ease tension, and restore balance. Research shows that techniques like this can reduce anxiety, support recovery after stress or surgery, and improve overall well-being (Aktaş & İlgin, 2023; Bentley et al., 2023; Luo et al., 2025).

How to do it

- Sit comfortably or lie down.
- Exhale fully through your mouth with a whoosh.
- Inhale through your nose for 4 seconds.
- Hold your breath for 7 seconds (without straining).
- Exhale slowly through your mouth for 8 seconds.
- Repeat for 3–4 cycles.
- Pause and notice how you feel.

You might also choose to add a grounding phrase as you breathe, such as: *In this moment, with this breath, all is well, and I am safe.* This phrase—often shared by one of our beloved somatic energy practitioners, Darlus Jonsson—offers a sense of reassurance that many find helpful.

Tips & Cautions

- Feeling lightheaded at first is normal—start slowly.
- If the full counts feel too long, shorten them while keeping the same ratio (inhale: hold: exhale).

This isn't about doing it perfectly—it's about creating calm, which includes letting go of the need to get it right.

Building Somatic Intelligence

As humans, we have a unique capacity for self-awareness, allowing us to observe not only our physical sensations like pain or tension, but also the thoughts and emotions that shape how we experience life. When we accept our emotions as a natural part of being human, we stop using energy to fight or avoid them. This frees us up to focus on the challenges in front of us, helping us become more resilient—better able to handle stress and change (Gilar-Corbi et al., 2025). By listening to the signals our bodies send us, we build **somatic intelligence**. This skill means understanding how our body and mind work together, which helps us feel more connected to ourselves and to others.

Figure 13 shows how emotions are typically felt in the body, reminding us of our shared humanity and helping normalize the interplay between emotions and physical sensations.

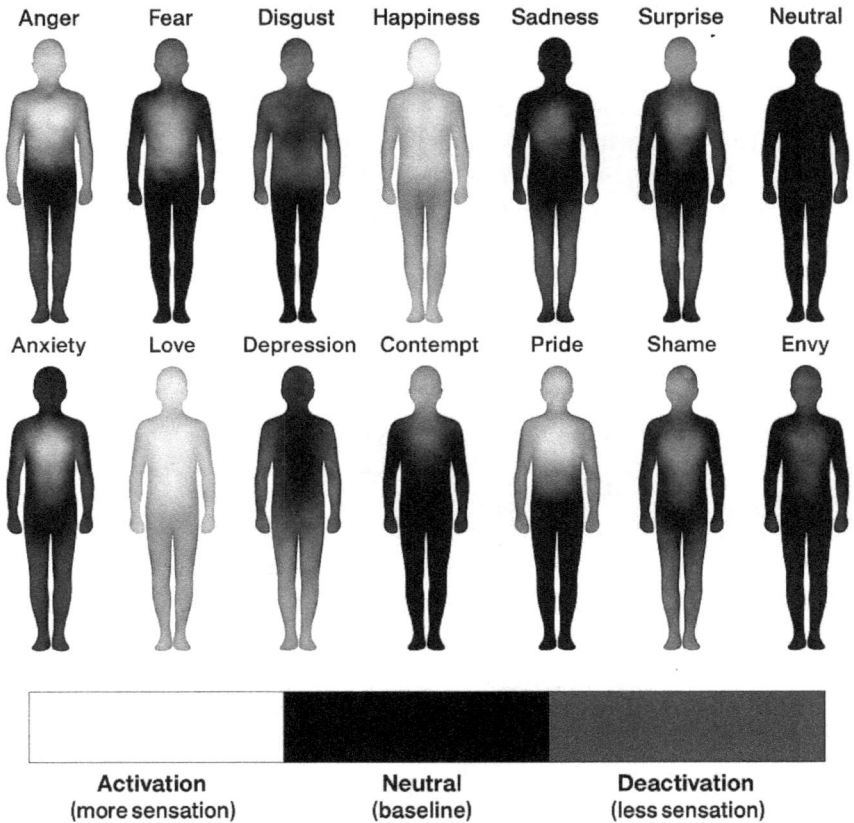

Figure 13. The body map shows regions where emotions tend to activate the body (Nummenmaa et al., 2018).

Framing Emotions as Phone Calls

Another way to frame our relationship with emotions is to imagine them as phone calls from our inner world. Each carries a message, trying to get our attention. When we answer the call—allowing ourselves to feel and process what's arising—we quiet the internal noise and create space to be fully present. When we ignore these calls, they don't stop ringing. They persist in the background, pulling our attention away from the moment and into cycles of stress or reactivity. By tuning in, we hear what our inner world is trying to say, and we free ourselves from the distraction of unprocessed emotional messages.

When emotional signals go unanswered for too long, the inner world can become increasingly noisy, creating chronic stress that dysregulates the nervous system. Over time, this persistent stress response can impair healing and elevate the risk of emotional and physical health problems, including depression and cardiovascular disease (Lei et al., 2025).

Rather than meeting this with shame about what we think we're doing wrong, we can turn toward self-compassion—recognizing that we arrived here for good reason, through protective mechanisms that helped us survive. The shift from surviving to thriving happens when the conditions are right. Creating those conditions opens space and grace to revisit the "voicemails" left by past experiences and begin answering the calls as they arise. For support in identifying which emotion is calling, refer to **Appendix A** for a list of emotional descriptors.

When we begin to answer emotional calls, we often discover that our responses are shaped by deeply instinctive patterns—rooted not in logic, but in the body's primitive nature. These protective responses—*fight, flight, freeze, or fawn*—are not flaws but signals from our nervous system, echoing the primal ways we've learned to stay safe. Across cultures, animals have long been honored as mirrors of these instinctive rhythms, offering insight into how we move through stress and how we might return to balance.

Pause to Practice: Relating emotions to our animal nature

Our nervous system is deeply primal—it carries patterns of protection that echo the animal world. When the body feels threatened, leading to the experience of stress, the reaction often comes from this instinctive protective place, moving us to fight, flee, hide, or adapt.

In many cultures, animals have long been honoured as teachers and guides, helping us see these instinctive patterns with compassion rather than judgment. Through their qualities, illustrated in **Figure 13,** we can begin to recognize the different ways our own 'animal nature' comes through.

Each of these protectors can show up under stress, but each also carries a gift when grounded and secure.

- **Turtle** → when insecure, avoids by retreating; when secure, carries the gift of patience and rest.
- **Ostrich** → when insecure, hides from reality; when secure, brings perspective and discernment.
- **Chameleon** → when insecure, disappears into the background; when secure, offers adaptability and sensitivity.
- **Wolf** → when insecure, projects onto others; when secure, embodies courage, loyalty, and strength.
- **Owl** → when insecure, withdraws into thought; when secure, carries wisdom and the ability to see in the dark.

When your body is experiencing stress, which animal spirit represented below tends to show up?

Which animal spirit quality would you like to invite more of?

Figure 13. Our 'animal nature' shows up in stress. Like owls, wolves, ostriches, turtles, and chameleons, we each have instinctive ways of coping with stress. By recognizing these patterns, we can better manage them.

WAYPOINT 7: LIVING WITH PURPOSE & MEANINGFUL ACTION

By this stage in the journey, life begins to make more sense, and a clearer sense of direction starts to emerge. Instead of drifting or reacting, we become more attuned to subtle patterns—bodily sensations, emotional shifts, and cues in our surroundings—that point us toward what matters most. These cues act as guideposts, helping us distinguish signal from noise, a concept introduced earlier. As we learn to recognize and follow them, our choices become more intentional, and our actions carry a deeper sense of meaning.

This process is supported by learning theory: our brains naturally prioritize cues that have previously led to meaningful outcomes—a phenomenon known as *the learned predictiveness effect* (Lee et al., 2024). As we become more sensitive to these signals, we're better able to identify what we call *significant actions*—small, intentional steps that align with both our inner truth and the external flow of life.

Neuroscience reinforces this understanding. The anterior cingulate cortex (ACC), introduced in *Waypoint 1*, helps us monitor outcomes and adjust behaviour when things don't go as expected, guiding us toward choices that feel congruent and purposeful (Huang et al., 2025).

As we gain confidence in following these internal signals, two primary resilience factors—sense of coherence and congruence—begin to strengthen. Sense of coherence grows as life feels more understandable, manageable, and meaningful. Congruence deepens as we live in greater alignment with our deeper calling, becoming more attuned to what resonates and what doesn't. Together, these shifts support a more resilient, intentional way of being.

Flow: When our actions are aligned with true nature

Dr. Crosbie Watler, serving as RTTs lead psychiatrist, frames flow through the teachings of yoga—emphasizing that it's not just the action, but the awareness within the action that matters:

> The term yoga is an ancient Sanskrit word that loosely translates to union. Union of body, mind and spirit. Spirit here refers to our essential and permanent self—the non-verbal, non-attached observer. The being that bears witness to the doing. In yoga, the doing (the pose) flows from awareness of breath, stepping out of the turnings of the mind. If we lose the awareness of breath, we are no longer in yoga, no matter how exquisite the pose.

Translating this practice into our daily lives, it's not the action alone that requires our attention, but also our awareness while in activity. *Are my actions arising solely from the constriction and conditioned patterns of the mind, or from the ease and stillness of our true nature, tethered to somatic intelligence and knowing?* If the latter, we are in flow, and in the domain of spontaneous and effortless right action.

Building on this insight, as we become more attuned to the subtle signals guiding our choices, a new quality of experience begins to emerge—one marked by *presence, ease,* and *alignment.* In these moments, action and awareness converge; time may feel suspended, and our movements arise effortlessly, as if carried by something greater than ourselves.

Seminal psychologist Mihaly Csikszentmihalyi (1975) described flow as a state that emerges when our skills are well matched to a challenge and when feedback arrives quickly and clearly. In flow, we don't need to consciously think through every step—*control shifts* from deliberate, effortful processes to more automatic ones. This creates a sense of moving with ease, confidence, and joy—what many describe as being carried by a larger rhythm.

Much like the winding path depicted in The Flow Path image, we navigate between states of boredom, apathy, anxiety, and exhaustion, finding that sweet spot where challenge and skill align. A surfer might call it *catching the wav*e, when balance and movement merge with the ocean's pulse. A jazz musician might call it *being in the pocket,* when improvisation flows through the body without strain. In all cases, flow arises when doing and being are no longer separate—when our actions are aligned with true nature.

Parts of the brain that help us focus, plan, and feel motivated—like areas in the prefrontal cortex—play an important role in flow states (Alameda et al., 2022). The ACC also helps by noticing when we're off track and bringing our attention back to what matters. Together, these systems help us sense when we're aligned, ease inner resistance, and make more room for clarity and presence.

Psychological and Universal Momentum

Momentum is what happens when we stop resisting life and begin to move with it. As we continue aligning our actions with our calling, life starts to feel less like a struggle and more like a collaboration. This doesn't mean challenges disappear; rather, we stop working against ourselves. Decisions feel guided rather than forced, and the environment seems more responsive.

Psychologists describe a related process called psychological momentum: the mind's natural tendency to carry forward thoughts and actions that fit with both current and future contexts (Honey et al., 2023). When we are aligned, this momentum propels us in a direction that feels both purposeful and supported—like a river current carrying us downstream, with our own strokes adding speed and direction rather than resistance.

In this way, learning isn't just a mental or cognitive activity. It becomes a spiritual unfolding—an ongoing process of discovering inner wisdom in harmony with the world around us. By recognizing cues, entering flow, and moving with momentum, we begin to see learning itself as a guidepost for living with purpose and meaningful action.

Significant Actions

Being a little off-balance isn't failure—it's feedback. It's the body's invitation to slow down, readjust, and return to rhythm.

Significant actions are intentional steps we take to anchor ourselves and regain a sense of control in times of uncertainty. It can be something small but meaningful—like taking a deep breath, reaching out to a friend, or choosing rest when we feel overwhelmed. These actions fortify our sense of integrity, agency, and courage, guiding us and enabling us to live in alignment with our values and calling.

When confronted with challenging circumstances, we find ourselves at a crossroads, offering a choice in our response. These responses may involve deciding on a specific course of action or intentionally refraining from action, allowing events to unfold naturally. Engaging in these deliberate actions empowers us to feel a sense of control amid uncertainty. This sense of empowerment is pivotal in elevating our overall sense of coherence, as discussed earlier, and contributes to our well-being. Moreover, it creates an environment conducive to inspired living. It's crucial to emphasize that for us to *be able* to take significant actions, the nervous system must feel secure enough to stand down (this is when self-soothing and regulation practices are helpful). Otherwise, we risk losing control to subconscious reactions, potentially derailing the possibility of an intentional response.

Order amid Chaos

Life can feel chaotic and unpredictable, especially in hard moments. By choosing what to do—or not to do—we create order from chaos, restoring a sense of control and confidence. Research supports this concept, showing that resilience grows when people use simple actions to cope with stress, like moving our body, breathing deeply, or doing small tasks, rather than staying passive (Hermans et al., 2025).

This order creates a stable foundation, enabling us to navigate turbulence with greater clarity. Moreover, our choices in response to challenges not only shape our immediate reality but also influence our long-term beliefs and memories of the situation. Actively taking part in significant actions allows us to mould our experiences, helping us move beyond unconscious reactions.

This proactive stance doesn't just affect the present outcome; it develops resilience, reinforcing our capacity to bounce back from adversity. These intentional choices serve as reminders of our inner strength, helping us develop a mindset of growth and learning in the face of life's storms.

Brain Science Behind Purposeful Action

When we choose to take purposeful action—like calming ourselves before reacting or planning our next step—we're using that part of the brain we referred to earlier, the anterior cingulate cortex (ACC). This plays a powerful role in helping us *notice* what's happening, *choose* how to respond, and *stay with it*—even when things are hard.

The ACC acts as a wise guide between thoughts, emotions, and actions. It helps us:

- **Notice inner conflict** (like when part of us wants to yell, but another part wants to stay calm),
- **Stay connected** to what matters most (like our values),
- **Focus attention** even when we're overwhelmed,
- **Stick with important goals**, even when progress feels slow.

When we pause to take a meaningful action—like a deep breath or reaching out for support—we activate the ACC, that region of the brain that is linked to resilience and goal-directed effort (Touroutoglou et al., 2020). Over time, strengthening the ACC enhances our ability to stay congruent with our true selves and deepens our sense of coherence—the feeling that life is manageable and meaningful.

Why it matters: Strengthening the ACC is like building a mental muscle that helps us find calm in chaos, courage in fear, and clarity when we feel stuck. When this part of our brain is active, we're more likely to feel that our actions are meaningful, that we have agency, and that we can grow through what we're going through.

Pause to Reflect: What does purposeful action look like?

Examples of significant actions can vary widely depending on the situation. Consider recent events, such as the ones provided below. *How might purposeful action help you navigate it more confidently?*

Conflict Scenario: Recall a recent disagreement with someone that led to lingering tension.

- **Action:** Instead of reacting impulsively, you pause, take a deep breath, and calmly express your feelings.
- **Result:** This intentional response helps ease the tension, opens the door to a more constructive dialogue, and supports healthier communication moving forward.

Overwhelm Scenario: Recall a situation where tasks felt overwhelming.

- **Action:** Implementing a significant action, like creating a prioritized to-do list adds a sense of order to the chaos of swirling tasks.
- **Result:** Reflect on how this planning might have provided a sense of order and control.

Fear Scenario: Think of a recent instance where you confronted a fear.

- **Action:** Envision choosing small, gradual steps as significant actions, adding order to the chaos that presents with uncertainty, through an intentional step-by-step process.
- **Result:** These intentional steps help us regain agency over emotions.

Incorporating significant actions into our lives necessitates a conscious shift from reactivity to proactivity. Through intentional choices guided by our inner healing intelligence, we develop trust in our abilities, which improves our sense of coherence. This trust becomes a cornerstone for navigating challenges with intention, resilience, and a renewed sense of control and confidence. This mindful practice gradually reshapes our interactions with the world, encouraging continuous personal growth and empowerment.

Remember, the journey of healing unfolds one moment at a time, followed by one inspired action at a time. As trust in our inner healing intelligence grows, the next right action becomes more obvious with time.

The Space Between Hope and Heartbreak

Optimism isn't denying pain—it's trusting our capacity to grow, turning challenges into invitations to evolve.

People who lean toward optimism experience much less stress than those who don't (Troy, 2015). An optimistic lens builds our confidence in handling challenges and strengthens our sense of coherence—the feeling that life is meaningful, understandable, and manageable.

Research shows that optimism helps people encounter fewer daily stressors and maintain greater emotional well-being across adulthood, shifting their overall emotional trajectory (Lee et al., 2022). Optimism is also linked with longevity—people who are more optimistic live, on average, 11 to 15% longer than those who are not (Lee et al., 2019).

Strategic optimism isn't helpful if it causes us to accept painful circumstances that are in our power to change, or if it's used to avoid feeling difficult emotions. In such cases, we may miss opportunities to tend to a wound that needs healing or to make necessary changes. As illustrated in the R.A.I.N.S. practice described earlier, *recognizing* our emotions and beliefs about the situation helps us understand our reaction. *Allowing* is an act of self-compassion, responding to our recognition. Part of *investigating* is noticing what's within our influence. Once the emotions have been tended to, a small, intentional action can sometimes help shift the energy that's been building. When change is possible, we gently acknowledge where we are and orient toward where we want to go. And when change isn't possible, the path naturally turns toward *nurturing* 'what is,' grieving what cannot be altered, and creating space for acceptance and healing.

Optimism is felt, not forced. A small internal shift can interrupt fear, restore perspective, and open space for possibility, reducing stress in the process.

Pause to Reflect: Grief as Love

Grief is love with no place to land.

Grief can arise with meaningful loss—including life's transitions and disappointments—when the heart keeps reaching for what once felt possible (Mikulincer & Shaver, 2016). Naming the loss is how we honour it. Taking a small, intentional action—whether it's lighting a candle, writing a note, sharing your story, saying a prayer, etc.—can help grief find a place to land, allowing what's yearning to move and transform. Consider how this might apply to you:

- What losses or transitions are present for you right now?
- Where's your heart still reach for what was/what might have been?
- What's a small action you could take to honour grief and help it land?

Working with Negative Bias

Because the brain is wired to focus more on the negative, we need to train ourselves to notice and savor the positive, helping to rebalance the mind toward optimism.

Most people tend to remember negative experiences more vividly than positive ones (Gollan et al., 2016). While this bias can be helpful in truly dangerous situations, it's less useful in everyday life. To shift this pattern, we can practice noticing and fully feeling positive moments. Over time, this helps retrain the brain to spot the good more easily, softening the grip of habitual negativity.

But leaning into optimism doesn't mean ignoring difficult emotions. If we rush to *look on the bright side*, we risk bypassing feelings that need to be felt to heal—like putting a Band-Aid on a deeper wound.

Emotions are messengers. They show up to guide us, not to harm us. When we stop labeling them as *good* or *bad*, we're less likely to see them as threats—and less likely to activate a stress response. Instead, we can welcome them as guests, allowing them to move through us.

Again, the goal isn't to avoid emotions, but to choose how long we stay in them. Neuroscientist Dr. Jill Bolte Taylor (2008) found that when we fully feel an emotion, its physical intensity usually lasts about 90 seconds. Each time we allow the emotional wave to fully pass through, we release stored emotional energy—lightening our load and opening the door to **transformation**, or even **transmutation**.

You could think of *transformation* as shaping our raw material—something unrefined, maybe even messy—and through intentional effort, we change its form into something functional and beautiful, like forming clay into a vase. In emotional terms, this process changes how we feel—like softening the edges of anxiety with breathwork or grounding practices. It doesn't erase the material; it reshapes it. It's about making a difficult emotional experience easier to hold and metabolize. *Transmutation* is alchemical. It's a complete change in the very essence of the emotional material. It's not just softening anxiety—it's turning the essence of suffering into wisdom, pain into purpose. This process often requires radical acceptance and deep inner work, like exposing lead to extreme heat until it becomes gold.

Where transformation helps us cope, transmutation helps us transcend. It's the deep work of taking something painful—like fear—and fundamentally changing it into compassion or wisdom. We give the emotion space to exist within us: *Pain, we see you, we hear you, we accept you, and we're right here with you*. This surrender releases the need to control or resist, freeing energy for the alchemical process. Through sustained practices of optimism, gratitude, and forgiveness—the emotional heat that melts old patterns—we forge a new, stronger reality.

Pause to Reflect: Transmuting with optimism

One way to shift from ruminating on what we can't control to optimistically reframing what we can is through the Serenity Prayer—a timeless reflection that offers not only comfort but also a pathway to **discernment**.

By helping us recognize the boundary between acceptance and purposeful action, it directs our energy toward what can truly make a difference. In doing so, it improves our sense of coherence—that belief that life is understandable, manageable, and meaningful.

> God, grant me the serenity to accept the things I cannot change,
> Courage to change the things I can,
> And wisdom to know the difference.
> —*Reinhold Niebuhr (c. 1932–1933, as cited in Brown, 1986)*

As you consider these words, think of a challenge in your life that can't be changed. Then, ask yourself: *What's within my power to shift?*

Sometimes, the most meaningful changes don't involve fixing the situation itself but rather adjusting how you relate to it. This might mean seeking support, redefining your role, or changing your expectations and perspective. For example, imagine dealing with a family member or coworker who consistently activates your nervous system. You may not be able to remove them from your life (this is what can't be changed), but you *can* influence how their behaviour affects you. By becoming curious about what action might help you feel more grounded, you open the door to transformation. This shift in perspective—viewing the situation through a different lens—can be powerful.

Often, when someone's behaviour stirs a strong reaction in us, it's because something in the present moment resonates with an old wound, as described in *Waypoint 2* as a projection. Our nervous system recognizes a familiar pattern and moves to protect us—sometimes before we even understand why. The person may feel like a threat, yet the reaction itself can provide information about where pain still lives in us. With support and curiosity, we can become aware of these echoes and tend to the feelings they awaken. Over time, this awareness helps loosen the hold of past experiences, creating space for greater freedom and choice in the future.

You may not have had the tools to process that pain when it first happened. But now, with more resources and awareness, the present-day activator becomes a teacher and an opportunity. You can listen to the message behind the emotion, release the energy that's been waiting to be felt, and lighten the load of stuck trauma you've been carrying.

Every release creates space—for breath, for choice, for connection. When the body no longer braces against the past, the heart begins to open toward relationship again. It's in our interactions with others that this healing becomes possible.

WAYPOINT 8: RELATIONAL ATTACHMENT PATTERNS

"We are all born so beautiful. The greatest tragedy is being convinced we are not."— *Rupi Kaur (n.d.)*

From our earliest moments, we begin learning how to relate to others—often without even realizing it—based on how our caregivers relate to themselves and to us. These early experiences shape the patterns we carry into adulthood, influencing how we seek closeness, handle conflict, and navigate emotional intimacy.

This Waypoint is an invitation to explore your attachment tendencies with curiosity and compassion. Rather than labeling or judging, we're simply noticing the ways we've learned to protect ourselves in relationships. These patterns aren't flaws—they're adaptive responses to the environments we grew up in. And here's the good news: they can change.

As you move through this section, you'll start to notice how your attachment patterns show up in everyday life—and how reconnecting with yourself through self-kindness and grounded awareness can support a shift toward more secure and authentic ways of relating. This is part of the journey toward congruence and a sustained sense of coherence: feeling safe enough to be yourself and resilient enough to meet life's challenges with clarity and creativity.

During childhood, we learn how to connect with others based on how our parents relate to themselves and to us (Bowlby, 2012). For example, if a parent struggles to provide a sense of safety, we might interpret it as rejection and seek connection elsewhere, sometimes appearing clingy or overly dependent. On the other hand, if a parent is emotionally intrusive or overly reliant on us, we might learn to avoid closeness, which can come across as distant or detached.

Attachment styles reflect the patterns we've developed in how we connect with others. Recognizing these tendencies allows us to interrupt old, unhelpful cycles. When our attachment patterns are out of sync, they often blend with the stress response and defensive behaviors. Feeling securely connected to ourselves and others begins with self-kindness. When we feel safe and grounded, we stop overthinking and can respond from a place of honesty and calm (*congruence*). From this centered place, we're better able to find meaning in challenges and respond with creativity and resilience (*sense of coherence*).

As shown in **Figure 14**, adults typically fall into one of three attachment styles—avoidant, secure, or anxious. The strength of our self-grounding influences how strongly these patterns show up in relationships.

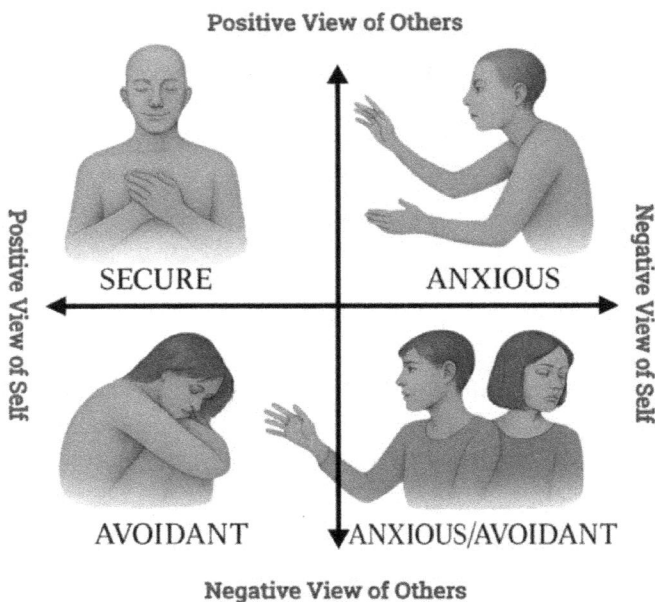

Positive View of Others

Positive View of Self — SECURE | ANXIOUS — **Negative View of Self**

AVOIDANT | ANXIOUS/AVOIDANT

Negative View of Others

Figure 14. Attachment tendencies in relation to one's view of self and others, adapted from attachment theory models.

Attachment tendencies aren't black and white—they're broad patterns with plenty of exceptions. Most of us fall somewhere along a spectrum, leaning toward either avoiding closeness or anxiously seeking it. Those with naturally secure attachments are actually in the minority—so we're in very good company. And remember: these labels aren't meant to box you in. They're simply tools to spark awareness, curiosity, and objectivity—qualities that help us work consciously with defensive behaviors that may not serve us well.

The good news? Attachment styles can change. When we start to recognize our patterns and the reactions they activate, we open the door to healing the distortions underneath. Many of us haven't experienced secure attachment with others—or even with ourselves. Learning what secure attachment feels like often begins by receiving it from others. Once we've felt it there, we can start cultivating it within. From that place, we can extend it outward—to our relationships, our children, and beyond. In this way, secure attachment can ripple through generations, reshaping old patterns.

Much like how we explored differentiating signal from noise in *Waypoint 6*, awareness of attachment tendencies helps us notice patterns that shape how we relate to others. Vogel's *Experiences in Close Relationships Scale* (Wei et al., 2007) is one widely used tool for measuring these tendencies, focusing on two dimensions: *attachment anxiety* and *avoidance*. The descriptors below are adapted from this research and expanded to include secure tendencies (Brown & Elliott, 2016), giving a fuller picture of the attachment spectrum.

80

Keep in mind: *these are tendencies—not fixed traits.* Depending on the relationship and what's happening inside us at any given moment, we can find ourselves anywhere along the spectrum. The goal isn't to label or limit us, but to spark awareness and curiosity, so we can respond with greater clarity and compassion.

Anxious tendencies:

- I need people to frequently reassure me.
- I seem to want to be closer to people than they do.
- Sometimes my desire to be close to people scares them away.
- I fear I'll be abandoned.
- I seem to care more about other people than they care about me.
- I feel frustrated when my partner isn't available when I need them.
- When it's time to say goodbye, I draw it out because I'm afraid to let go.

Avoidant tendencies:

- I rarely turn to others, even those close to me, in times of need.
- I long for close relationships, but I instinctively pull back.
- I don't rely on others for reassurance.
- I keep one foot outside the door of relationships most of the time.
- I avoid getting too close to others; it makes me uneasy.
- I enjoy the intensity of a new relationship but often withdraw after a while.
- I don't usually share my real problems with others.
- I prefer quick transitions—I don't like drawn-out goodbyes.

Secure tendencies (Brown & Elliott, 2016):

- I feel safe and protected.
- I am supported to be my best self.
- I am seen, known, and understood.
- When hurt, I am soothed and comforted.
- Just by being myself, I am delightful.

Pause to Reflect: What are your attachment tendencies?

As you read through the descriptors above, notice what patterns feel most familiar to you.

- When you think about past or current relationships, can you notice any subtle shifts in those patterns?
- How might your environment or the people around you be shaping the way you respond?

It's natural to want to externalize our patterns—blaming the situation or the other person—but often, our reactions have more to do with past experiences than the present moment. These responses can serve as cues, pointing to old wounds that may need care. The person in front of us usually isn't the source of the pain; it's often tied to protective parts shaped by past wounds, sensing something familiar. Meeting these parts with awareness and compassion is a powerful opportunity to rewire our nervous system—softening the places where we tend to react and creating space for discernment and choice.

In short, just because we don't like the version of ourselves that shows up in certain relationships doesn't necessarily mean we need to leave them. Instead, it can often be an opportunity to grow awareness within the relationship— learning to notice, pause, and respond with greater clarity and compassion.

Much like how we explored *differentiating signal from noise* in *Waypoint 6*, awareness of attachment tendencies helps us learn to discern when a situation is inviting us to turn inward—allowing the outer world to serve as a teacher— and when changes in the outer world are necessary for our safety and growth.

Attachment Antidotes: Navigating relationships with choice

Attachment antidotes are tools that help us shift old, automatic patterns in relationships. They're also the *significant actions* described in the final step of R.A.I.N.S.—intentional choices that restore our sense of agency.

By consciously applying these antidotes, we move beyond reactive habits that no longer serve us. This empowers us to make thoughtful decisions, fostering secure connections with ourselves and others. Over time, this process strengthens congruence and a sense of coherence, building the self-compassion and inner stability needed to set honest boundaries and feel safe in relationships.

For Anxious Attachment: Build self-trust

Antidote = REACH IN

If you tend to feel anxious in relationships, you might often seek reassurance or fear disconnection. This can lead to focusing more on others than on your own inner world.

A powerful antidote is to **build self-trust**—learning to connect with your own feelings, sensations, and needs. By tuning into your emotional cues with curiosity instead of fear, you begin to see them as messengers rather than threats. This shift takes practice, but it's foundational to developing a secure attachment to yourself.

It also helps to diversify your support system, so your emotional needs aren't reliant on just one or two people.

For Avoidant Attachment: Practice vulnerability

Antidote = REACH OUT

If you tend to keep others at a distance, healing involves taking small risks to express your needs and emotions. These acts of vulnerability—naming your boundaries, sharing your truth—are key to building trust and mutual connection.

Even when it feels uncomfortable, prioritizing honest self-expression helps create a secure foundation in relationships. Over time, this opens the door to deeper, more reciprocal bonds.

Note: Before we *pause to practice*, it's important to remember that difficulty accessing compassion or secure attachment often stems from early relational trauma. These patterns are protective, not pathological. Healing begins with recognizing that these responses were once necessary—and that, with safety and support in consistently trustworthy relationships, they can begin to soften. For many of us, these protective patterns formed over years, even decades. Developing trust, therefore, takes time—however long it takes to test and experience the environment as truly safe.

Pause to Practice: Applying attachment antidotes

Recognizing our attachment tendencies is the first step toward healing, but awareness alone isn't enough. To shift these patterns, we need intentional practices that help us respond differently—especially in moments of stress or disconnection. These practices, which we call attachment antidotes, help us meet our *selves* with understanding and compassion. Whether we're reaching inward to build self-trust or reaching outward to practice vulnerability, these small, meaningful actions help us move from protection to connection.

Let's bring this into lived experience. Think back to a recent situation that felt stressful or emotionally charged—perhaps a conflict or moment of disconnection.

- How might you approach it differently now?
- Which antidote—REACH IN or REACH OUT—could help shift your response?
- What might change if you applied that antidote?

You don't need to wait for the next challenge to practice. Try *visualizing* a new response. Just like athletes use mental rehearsal to improve performance, imagining yourself responding with calm and clarity activates many of the same brain pathways as actually doing it. This approach strengthens new habits and makes it easier to apply them in real life.

Remember, growth is a process. Be gentle with yourself. Pushing too hard or too fast can lead to overwhelm. Instead, take a *slow and steady* approach, guided by self-compassion. Each small step helps you build the capacity for more secure, authentic relationships.

To begin shifting our attachment patterns, we can start by offering ourselves the kind of secure connection we may have longed for. The following affirmations help us understand and eventually embody that sense of safety and belonging.

Pause to Practice: Cultivating secure attachment

Here, we offer affirmations embodying the five beliefs characteristic of a secure child and adult (Brown & Elliott, 2016). Speaking these affirmations with your own words and voice, addressing yourself as you would a *dear other*, can help it feel more authentic. Imagine the warmth and protection you'd extend to a *dear other* and speak the affirmations from that tender place.

Affirmations for Secure Attachment:

- I am secure and protected.
- I am encouraged to be my authentic self.
- I am deserving of being seen, known, and understood.
- When hurting, I am worthy of comfort and solace.
- I am enough, just as I am.

Take a moment to reflect:

How did this exercise feel for you?

As you recited these affirmations, what sensations did you notice in your body?

When we practice security, we teach the nervous system a new language of safety. Eventually, that language becomes our own inner voice—a tone of kindness that guides us home when we've strayed into self-criticism or shame.

In the next Waypoint, we'll explore how this internalization of care translates to self-compassion—the practice of holding ourselves with the same warmth we offer to those we love.

WAYPOINT 9: SELF-COMPASSION

Self-compassion is the medicine that helps us return to ourselves when we feel most lost. It's not something we force—it's something we learn in our relationships. We learn self-kindness through the kindness of others. Community makes that possible. In spaces where unconditional positive regard is consistently mirrored, we start to trust that we may indeed be worthy, which loosens the grip of self-judgement. Eventually, as we learn the tune of it, we become able to turn it inward.

What's Self-Compassion?

True self-compassion means being kind to ourselves—even and especially when we feel imperfect or unsuccessful. It's about offering unconditional positive regard inward, especially during moments of struggle or when we make mistakes—like the way we'd treat a close friend, with care, patience, and understanding (Neff & Germer, 2018; Benedetto et al., 2024).

We learn self-compassion through relationships where we're accepted just as we are. When others meet us with warmth and acceptance, we begin to believe we're worthy of that kindness. Over time, we internalize this experience and learn to extend it to ourselves (Rogers, 1959; Brown & Elliott, 2016).

Self-compassion helps us feel safe and grounded. It calms the nervous system during times of stress, reducing anxiety and depression, while increasing joy, confidence, and emotional resilience (Bluth et al., 2017; Gunnell et al., 2017; Homan & Sirois, 2017; Hwang et al., 2016; Kelly et al., 2014; Dames, 2018). Living with integrity—choosing actions aligned with our values rather than driven by fear—is one way we practice self-compassion (Wong et al., 2025).

The Inner Landscape

The following image illustrates *the shift from the inner critic to the inner nurturer*—a process described by Neff (2003) as the cultivation of self-compassion through three interrelated components.

- Through mindfulness, we learn to recognize our suffering without over-identifying with it.
- Through common humanity, we remember that struggle and imperfection are universal experiences rather than personal shortcomings.
- Through self-kindness, we respond to ourselves with warmth and care instead of criticism.

MINDFULNESS

COMMON HUMANITY

SELF-KINDNESS

INNER CRITIC

INNER NURTURER

Each step moves us toward an inner stance of compassion—transforming judgment into understanding and disconnection into belonging.

Through the practice of self-compassion, we can **transform** our relationship with suffering—shifting from resistance to understanding. Over time, this awareness **transmutes** pain itself, allowing the same energy that once contracted the heart to become a source of wisdom and connection. Compassion doesn't erase difficulty; it changes its texture, softening the edges until what was once unbearable becomes tenderly human.

What Gets in the Way?

What often gets in the way is *conditional self-compassion*—being kind only when we're trying to fix something or feel better fast. This approach doesn't last. When we don't feel good enough, we often try to prove our worth through hustling for perfection, which fuels scarcity, stress, and shame (Benedetto et al., 2024). Our lived experiences and societal influences can pull us away from our authentic selves, reinforcing the belief that our identity is tied to our story. This conditionality locks us into a cycle of insecurity and disconnection— where we chase external validation, turning down the volume of internal distress signals, in an effort to preserve a sense of belonging, one of our most fundamental human needs for survival. Shame arises from this misalignment—what Carl Rogers called *incongruence*—reminding us we've lost touch with who we are.

Coping mechanisms—like people pleasing, food, sex, substances, screen time, or shopping—can be seen not as disorders, but as coping responses to trauma and disconnection. These patterns reflect a common root, and healing begins by addressing that root from the inside out.

Pause to Reflect: What story of self are you living by?

This reflection provides a moment to check in, not to judge or evaluate—just notice what's here within you right now.

How do you feel about yourself as a person?

Rather than answering with a single word or label, consider where you typically fall along these gradients of inner experience—not as a judgment, but as a way to notice how you relate to yourself over time.

- I often feel harsh or critical toward myself.
- I tend to doubt or minimize my own worth.
- I'm learning to meet myself with understanding, even when I fall short.
- I can often offer myself kindness and encouragement.
- I feel at home with myself, even in moments of challenge.

Take a moment to notice how this inner voice shifts depending on where you are and who you're with.

How does it sound when you're alone, compared to when you're with people who truly see and accept you? What helps that voice soften—and what tends to make it tighten?

As you reflect, notice how your environment and relationships shape your sense of safety and belonging. Some spaces and people make it easy to feel free and open, while others we may notice our guard is consistently up. Having this awareness doesn't mean we can change everything right away—but it helps us recognize how the environments and relationships we are surrounded by matter.

Neuroscience suggests that our brains are wired for resonance: through mirror neurons, we unconsciously reflect the emotional states, tone, and body language of those around us. Recent research shows that these networks support empathy and emotional regulation, helping us internalize the rhythms and safety of the environments we inhabit (Bonini et al., 2022). In supportive relationships, this resonance strengthens our sense of coherence and calm. Over time, our being consistently met with acceptance can reshape the internal dialogue we carry.

Acting on this awareness, we become more resourced and able to make choices that align with who we are becoming. We spend more time in relationships that nurture us and step back, when possible, from those that reinforce fear or self-doubt. In this way, awareness opens the door to creating the conditions necessary for change.

Pause to Practice: Finding a friend in our *Selves*

Most of us don't move through life with just one steady inner voice. We're shaped by many parts—the tender ones, the tired ones, the brave ones, and the ones that simply need a break. Each Self is doing its best to protect us, guide us, or make sense of what's happening.

When we talk about *finding a friend in our Selves*, we're naming this inner landscape. Many of us are skilled at criticizing these parts, while befriending them can feel unfamiliar. Yet this shift matters. It moves us from "something is wrong with me" to "I can care for myself differently." It's the movement from surviving to thriving—becoming a steady, compassionate mirror for each Self, even those that don't always show up in their best form. This practice helps us meet that inner presence and begin building a relationship with it.

We've explored how our inner voice changes with what's around us—and how our relationships shape our sense of safety and belonging. The practice that follows turns that awareness toward our inner landscape.

One of the gentlest ways to soften self-talk is to speak to ourselves as we would to someone dear to us.

Start by bringing to mind someone you deeply care about—someone whose heart you understand, someone you'd show up for without hesitation. Imagine they've come to you in a tender moment, feeling overwhelmed or uncertain, and they're seeking a little comfort or clarity.

What would you say to help them feel safe, understood, and not alone?

It might sound something like:

Hey, my friend. I know this is really hard, and it makes sense that you feel this way. You're doing the best you can with what you have right now—and that is more than enough. Simply noticing what you're feeling takes courage. I'm right here with you.

Now flip the perspective for a moment. Imagine *you* were the one hearing those words from someone you trust, someone who truly cares about you.

How would it feel to receive that kind of kindness? What would soften inside you?

The next time you're having a hard moment, try finding a quiet place and offering yourself the same tone you'd naturally use with a dear friend. It doesn't have to be perfect. Just heart-led and honest.

Building our Self-Compassion Muscles

Self-care means different things to different people. For some, it offers permission to be kind to themselves. For others, it can feel like a chore or even selfish. But the moment self-care becomes a task we *should* do—driven by obligation rather than desire—it stops being self-compassion. In fact, it can become counterproductive and even harmful (Barnett & Homany, 2023).

Self-compassionate care is guided by what feels nurturing, not by what looks good from the outside. It's less about ticking off a to-do list and more about tuning into the needs of the body, heart, and spirit.

As Helen Watler, our lead somatic energy practitioner, often reminds us to ask:

How do you want to feel right now?

This question helps us pause, tune in, and accept what's here—before we even think about changing it. Real transformation doesn't come from forcing; it grows from the ground of acceptance and inspiration. When we allow what is, without judgment, space opens for something new to emerge.

From this place of acceptance, the question deepens: *How do I want to feel?* Not how we think we *should* feel, but what our body and heart are genuinely longing for. That longing—so often dismissed as selfish—is usually the body naming what it needs to feel whole.

When we listen and respond with care, we begin to build trust with ourselves. Attending to how we want to feel supports emotional regulation, resilience, and self-compassion (Neff, 2003; Lindsay et al., 2019). Over time, we learn to stand more and more on our own side. And when we tend to ourselves first, we don't take away from others—we actually have more to give. A full cup spills over naturally. Empirical evidence supports this point as well: those who practice self-compassion demonstrate greater prosocial behaviour toward others, suggesting that self-kindness enhances rather than reduces our capacity for generosity (Liu et al., 2025).

To experience this directly, let's practice offering compassion to our nervous system—one of our most loyal allies. It works tirelessly to keep us safe and balanced. By extending kindness inward, we interrupt habitual patterns of resistance and create space for regulation and ease.

Pause to Practice: Compassion for the nervous system

Earlier, we explored what it's like to offer friendship to our *selves*. The nervous system, though different from our *selves*, responds to the same steady presence. If the Selves are like the kids in the family, the nervous system is the parent who loves them fiercely, worries a lot, and sometimes prepares for storms that aren't actually coming. It doesn't do this to scare us—it does it because, somewhere along the way, it learned that staying alert was the safest way to survive.

When we can see our nervous system through this lens—not as something broken, but as a devoted protector that's sometimes a little overactive or confused—compassion naturally softens the way we meet our internal experience. Awareness begins to arise from a place of abundance rather than fear. From here, unconditional positive regard can turn inward, and we slowly begin to trust that we are, in fact, enough.

Understanding that the nervous system is always trying to help us, we can start meeting its stress responses with kindness instead of judgment or self-blame.

One way to do this is to speak to these reactions the way you might speak to a dear other: with warmth, clarity, and a bit of healthy distance—much like setting a kind boundary so you can walk alongside a friend without getting swept up in their experience. When activated, we might ask, *what would feel soothing to hear right now?* This practice helps us grow a steadier, more compassionate inner voice.

Here are a few examples of how you might speak to your nervous system with that same caring, grounded presence:

To the protective parts of your nervous system:

- *I really appreciate how hard you've worked to protect me.*
- *You stepped in when I didn't know how to protect myself. I'm safe now, and I can handle things.*
- *I see how much you've done to keep me safe. You've been a loyal friend.*
- *We're not alone now. We're in a safer place.*

To the parts carrying fear or hurt from earlier in life:

- *I recognize your pain. I feel it too.*
- *I'm so sorry you had to go through that.*
- *I'm here with you now. You're not facing this alone.*
- *We can move through this together.*

If it helps, imagine someone you deeply care about—a child, grandparent, partner, friend, or parent—in a moment of vulnerability. *How would you offer them warmth and reassurance?* You can use that very same tone.

Try experimenting with different ways of speaking to yourself and see what feels comforting or grounding. Over time, you'll begin to discover a voice within that feels familiar—a voice that feels like home. And in doing so— simply witnessing what's here with compassion, especially when it's different from what we wish it was—we direct unconditional positive regard inward.

Re-Parenting and Re-Partnering Dislocated Parts

People who grow up surrounded by unconditional positive regard often carry a natural sense of self-compassion into adulthood. But for many of us, early environments didn't offer that kind of acceptance—and the result is that it can feel unsafe or unfamiliar to turn unconditional positive regard inward.

When attuned care was missing, parts of us can remain dislocated—stuck in old protective patterns, still scanning for danger, unsure if the world will respond with kindness. These wounds don't disappear with time. They surface in moments of stress or vulnerability, asking to be seen, understood, and integrated. Our inner healing intelligence doesn't bring these parts up to throw us off balance—it does so because it's always holding the bigger picture.

So, if the *selves* are like the kids in the family, these dislocated parts are often the ones who were most frightened or overlooked—the kids who learned to protect themselves in whatever way they could. And just as the nervous system acts like an overprotective parent, doing its best to keep everyone safe, these younger selves often misread the present through the lens of an unsafe past.

As we learn to re-parent and re-partner these younger selves, we're also rewiring the nervous system itself. With time and compassion, it can shift from being an overprotective, anxious guardian to a grounded protector—one that watches over the parts without overwhelming them. In this way, the nervous system can be honoured for its loyalty without feeling threatening to the very parts it's trying to keep safe.

To truly heal, we don't force these parts to change—we call them home with compassion. This is the heart of re-parenting and re-partnering. As the resourced adults we are now, we can offer the warmth, steadiness, and attunement we may not have received earlier in life. We return to these inner wounds with the presence of someone who finally knows how to listen.

Through re-parenting and re-partnering, we start to:

- Acknowledge these parts as unhealed wounds—not flaws, threats, or failures.
- Feel them fully, once we create enough spaciousness to know they are part of us, but not the whole of us.
- Nurture them with unconditional positive regard, offering the care that was missing.

With each encounter, we reclaim a piece of our deeper self—the parts that once felt unsafe, unwanted, or unlovable. Every time an intense emotion rises, we're given an invitation: to sit with these younger Selves, to hold space for what they carry, and to remind them that they are no longer alone.

This is how we bring all of our selves home.

Pause to Practice: Applying R.A.I.N.S. to insecure parts

The following practice supports us in bringing this compassionate tone into our lived experience, meeting insecurity with presence rather than judgment. As we enter the practice, let these words remind us of our inherent worth— the knowing that every part of us belongs.

> You are a child of the universe
> no less than the trees and the stars;
> you have a right to be here.
> And whether or not it is clear to you,
> no doubt the universe is unfolding as it should.
> — M. Ehrmann, *Desiderata* (1927/2023)

This excerpt by Max Ehrmann, a historic American poet and philosopher, offers timeless wisdom—reminding us that each part of ourselves has an inherent right to exist.

While we often judge or suppress the parts that feel insecure, these are the ones most in need of compassionate attention. They have been shaped by early conditions where their needs weren't met—and they still carry the imprint of those painful experiences.

It bears repeating: *every part belongs*. Each was shaped by love or longing, and each deserves to rest in your acceptance. These parts come to the surface of awareness when the environment—and our nervous system—are safe enough to receive them.

R.A.I.N. offers a way to meet them with care, transforming avoidance into connection:

- **R**ecognize when you're being hard on yourself.
- **A**llow the experience to be present without judgment.
- **I**nvestigate with curiosity—*what part of you is hurting or afraid?*
- **N**urture yourself with compassion, offering the same care you would give a dear friend.

This perspective helps foster non-attachment by allowing you to witness your experience with kindness rather than over-identifying with it.

Adding the **S** to R.A.I.N.—the **Significant Action**—is a powerful way to reinforce agency and intentional action. It becomes the bridge between insight and embodiment. So, consider one small, intentional step. This could be an action, a boundary, a pause, or even a mindset shift. The goal isn't to fix or rush, but to reclaim a sense of choice and direction.

Significant action isn't about pushing forward—it's about noticing when the body feels safe enough to take a small, meaningful step.

Examples of Significant Actions:

- Saying no to something that feels misaligned and celebrating the courage it took.
- Reaching out to someone who offers unconditional positive regard.
- Writing a note to yourself from your inner healer.
- Taking a walk in nature to reconnect with your body and breath.
- Practicing a grounding breath before responding to an activating situation.
- Reframing a limiting belief with a more compassionate truth.
- Choosing to rest instead of pushing through exhaustion.
- Creating a small ritual to honour your growth (e.g., lighting a candle, journalling, stretching).

These actions don't need to be big—they just need to be meaningful. Each one strengthens your ability to respond rather than react, helping you come to trust that—as Ehrmann reminds us—even when it isn't clear, the universe is unfolding *as it should*.

Each small act of compassion—each moment of choosing presence over judgment—gradually restores trust within. As we practice meeting ourselves with care, something begins to shift: the walls of protection soften, and what once felt unworthy of love begins to relax into belonging.

From this place of kindness, we can begin to listen more deeply to what these tender parts are holding. Having learned to meet them with care, we now turn to practices that lighten the burdens they carry—the stories, griefs, and defences that once kept us safe but now weigh us down.

And as we do, another expression of self-compassion naturally unfolds: **forgiveness**—a softening that follows meeting pain with acceptance and care.

Forgiveness: A Rhythm of Care

Forgiveness, much like self-compassion, calls us to tend the body's wounds with tenderness. It doesn't dismiss harm or imply that what occurred was okay—it gently releases the hold of painful narratives so we can reclaim our energy, clarity, and peace. Forgiveness is not a single choice but a rhythm of care—an embodied, gradual process of returning to ourselves.

Research shows that forgiveness—especially when it reduces unforgiveness— is linked to improved mental and physical health. Rumination and reflection are key mediators in this relationship, suggesting that forgiveness interrupts cycles of mental rehearsal that perpetuate suffering (Mróz & Kaleta, 2023). Similarly, non-attachment—the ability to step back from painful narratives, so we can respond with clarity and compassion—increases psychological flexibility and reduces emotional distress (Sahdra et al., 2010). When resentment lingers, the body may remain in a chronic state of activation, undermining our well-being (Kelly, 2018).

Forgiveness isn't about forgetting or condoning harm—it's about reclaiming the energy that resentment consumes. When past wounds remain open and untended, we become tethered to ongoing pain that shapes our emotions, behaviours, and relationships. In doing so, a piece of our freedom is lost—the freedom to live fully in the present, unburdened by the past.

Pause to Reflect: What are you *giving* your freedom *for*?

Elder Duncan Grady asks, "*What are you willing to give—for your freedom?*" (personal communication, September 2022)

This question invites us to consider what we're still carrying, and whether we're ready to release it in exchange for peace.

Consider a past wound and the resentment you may still carry. *How does this wound continue to take up space in your day-to-day life—through emotions, projections, or behaviours?*

As you reflect, remember that forgiveness is less an act of will and more a gradual unfolding.

Forgiveness as a Practice of Unfolding

Forgiveness doesn't require closure or resolution—it asks only for willingness, and for the conditions that allow softening to begin.

Forgiveness rarely arrives in a single moment of clarity. It unfolds in layers— through repeated invitations to soften, to feel, and to release. The body, shaped by its history, may resist this process at first. It may need time to trust that it's safe enough to let go.

This is why forgiveness resembles tending a deep wound—one that needs time, steady care, and supportive conditions to heal from within. A bandage alone can't bring resolution; covered without attention, a wound may fester. Forgiveness asks us to keep the wound open to healing—safeguarded from new harm but given space to breathe. It moves us to cultivate the conditions that let healing unfold naturally, at the pace the process requires.

While forgiveness doesn't change the past, it transforms how we relate to it. Without it, past wounds can bleed into the present, causing us to misattribute our suffering to current events and relationships.

When the body feels safe enough, forgiveness may begin to reshape how we remember—softening the emotional charge and allowing new meaning to emerge. Though the facts remain, our role can shift from victim to victor. This shift disrupts sticky thought patterns and allows us to move forward without re-experiencing past violations. In recognizing the lessons within these experiences, suffering can transform into wisdom.

Forgiveness may begin with a whisper of willingness—a softening that arises when the body senses it's safe enough to feel. It may involve naming the pain, acknowledging the impact, and creating space for grief, anger, or sorrow to move through. It's not about bypassing emotion but about making room for it to be felt and metabolized.

Over time, as the body learns it's safe to let go, forgiveness becomes a form of integration—a way of honouring what has been lost while reclaiming what remains. It's a gesture of care toward the self, and toward the nervous system that has worked so hard to protect us.

Before moving into the practice of forgiveness, you might ask yourself: *What am I still holding onto, and am I ready—just a little—to begin softening my grip?*

As we come to see forgiveness not as a single act but as a rhythm—a process that unfolds in its own time—we can begin to explore what it feels like in practice. What follows isn't a prescription or a checklist; it's an invitation to be with your breath, your body, and your heart in the slow work of letting go. If you feel well-resourced, you're welcome to continue. If not, that's okay—honour where you are. This practice will still be here when you're resourced and ready.

Pause to Practice: Tending the wound with forgiveness

This practice is best approached when the body feels supported and the nervous system is relatively settled. Forgiveness asks us to be present with what hurts, and that requires a foundation of safety. If you're not ready, that's okay. You can return to this practice whenever the conditions feel right.

Begin by *Recognizing* what's present—naming the sensations, emotions, or memories arising, and meeting them with acceptance. Continuing with the R.A.I.N. model, we then *Allow* what's here to be here; *Inquire* with curiosity and non-attachment, and *Nurture* what arises with compassion.

To create a greater sense of safety, focus on making space rather than identifying with the pain. Try speaking to your body as you would to a dear friend—acknowledging its efforts to protect you and inviting it to soften. This relational stance signals safety to the nervous system, making space to lean in without the usual defenses standing in the way.

Let's begin the practice:

- **Settle into your body.** Take a few deep breaths. Feel your feet on the ground. Let your shoulders drop.
- **Bring someone to mind.** This may be yourself or someone else—someone toward whom you feel lingering resentment, shame, or regret.
- **Visualize them sitting across from you.** See them not as their actions, but as a human being who has also suffered. If it's yourself, imagine your younger self—perhaps the version of you who was doing the best they could with what they had.
- **Speak to the body with care.** You might say, *I see you've been holding this for a long time. Thank you for protecting me.* This helps the body feel safe enough to soften.
- **Breathe compassion.** Inhale into your heart space. Exhale compassion toward them. If it helps, imagine a soft light moving between you.
- **Repeat the following phrases, aloud or silently.** These are adapted from a Buddhist-inspired forgiveness prayer commonly shared in meditation and mindfulness settings (Interfaith Prayers, n.d.):

95

If I have harmed anyone in any way, either knowingly or unknowingly, through my own confusion, I ask their forgiveness.

If anyone has harmed me in any way, either knowingly or unknowingly, through their confusion, I forgive them.

If there is something I am not yet ready to forgive, I forgive myself for that.

For all the ways I harm myself—through doubt, judgment, or unkindness—I forgive myself.

Notice what shifts. You may feel lighter. You may feel emotional. You may feel nothing at all. All responses are valid. Remembering that forgiveness is more of a process than a destination.

If it feels right, you might close with gratitude—for your presence, for your body's protection, and for the process that's *slowly* unfolding.

As Elder Duncan Grady reminds us, forgiving ourselves for what we didn't yet know is often the hardest kind (personal communication, March 2023). Yet when we offer ourselves the same grace we would extend to a dear friend, we begin to loosen the grip of shame and open the door to healing.

As the practice closes, you may notice subtle shifts—perhaps a softening, a release, or simply presence.

Whatever arises, it belongs. Forgiveness isn't a one-time event—it's a rhythm we return to. And as that rhythm takes root, another layer of healing comes into view: **repair**. Forgiveness frees the heart, but repair restores the bridge between us.

Repair as Path

Repair is about rebuilding trust where it has been strained or lost. It asks us to show up with humility, compassion, and a willingness to take responsibility. Rather than seeing ruptures as failures, we can understand them as *signals* that something in the shared relational space needs attention—whether that's clearer boundaries, clearer consent, or a return to respect.

Because "skid outs" are inevitable—inside ourselves and with others—repair becomes part of our evolution. Each time we meet tension with curiosity rather than defensiveness, we strengthen our capacity for connection and grow in awareness.

Repair Begins Within

When harm happens, repair will eventually include an apology—but the apology is *not* the starting point. It needs to come *after* we've gone inward.

Elder Duncan Grady offers a teaching about this:

"It's better to go in and down than up and out, though the latter is far more seductive."
(personal communication, March 2023)

"Going in and down" means pausing long enough to feel the impact, acknowledge what's ours, and soften the impulse to protect ourselves. Without this inner work, apologies tend to be rushed or defensive—more about escaping discomfort than rebuilding trust.

The "up and out" path—blame, justification, avoidance, or spiritual bypass—may feel easier in the moment, but it usually widens the rupture. Turning inward prepares us to return with honesty, steadiness, and genuine care.

Motivation and Follow-Through Matter

Research shows that repair is most effective when it comes from a sincere desire to mend the relationship rather than from pressure or self-protection (Brandmayr, 2021). And follow-through matters too—not as self-sacrifice, but as meaningful action that reflects integrity. Without this grounding, even a beautifully worded apology can feel hollow or performative (DiFonzo et al., 2020).

For the person who has been hurt, repair is not just about the words spoken—it's about trusting that the harm won't happen again. Re-entering relationship is vulnerable; sincerity and consistency make that vulnerability feel safer.

When Repair Meets Forgiveness

These practices prepare us for the harder conversations and help us show up with more clarity and compassion. Still, repair alone isn't always enough. Forgiveness brings its own medicine. It softens the grip of hurt and creates space for trust to grow again. Forgiveness is relational—supported by empathy, closeness, and the sincerity of our efforts to make things right (Folmer et al., 2021).

When repair and forgiveness find each other, something shifts. The weight of the rupture begins to lift, and space opens for **grace**—a quiet presence that meets us where we are and supports who we are becoming.

Moving in Grace

Forgiveness clears a path by loosening the grip of resentment and softening the pain of past wounds. Yet what often follows is something more elusive—a gentle presence that meets us in the space that's opened. This is the work of *grace:* the unearned gift that meets us as we are and carries us toward who we are becoming. Research affirms this, describing grace as a transformative force that enhances human flourishing by offering acceptance and renewal beyond what effort alone can achieve (Emmons et al., 2017).

A verse from the *Therīgāthā*, composed by early Buddhist elder nuns, expresses this state of release and purity:

> Like a blue lotus rising from the water,
> unsmeared by the mud it grows in—
> so am I freed, unsmeared by the world.
> — *trans. B. Sujato, c. 6th–3rd century BCE*

This image of the lotus—rooted in the mud yet untouched by it—reminds us that grace arises not from escaping life, but from meeting it with clarity and compassion. Interconnection begins here: in the still lake of awareness where self and world meet as one continuous breath.

Grace can arrive through relationships, nature, or spiritual encounter—meeting us in our most vulnerable places with compassion. It softens the grip of shame and self-judgment, creating space for clarity and courage. Research on self-compassion and acceptance shows that these experiences increase resilience and psychological flexibility (Neff & Germer, 2018; Garland et al., 2015). Grace, then, is less about striving and more about surrender. It emerges from trusting that transformation unfolds not through force, but through allowing ourselves to be met, lifted, and carried beyond where we began.

A sense of ease grows when the body feels safe enough to soften—not through effort, but through the conditions that allow release. Research supports this view: people who loosen rigid beliefs about themselves, rather than clinging to who they think they should be, feel more balanced, less stressed, and more at ease (Whitehead et al., 2018).

Letting go isn't about abandoning ourselves—it's about holding ourselves differently. With tenderness. With spaciousness. With trust in the body's innate capacity to heal when met with care.

Grace whispers what effort can't: healing comes when we soften, not when we push harder. The *Butterfly Hug* offers a way to experience that tenderness in the body—holding ourselves with the same compassion we might offer another.

Pause to Practice: Self-holding with the 'butterfly hug'
Adapted from Artigas et al. (2000)

This practice can invite calm into the body and cultivate a sense of safety and presence. Developed by psychologist Lucina Artigas in response to collective trauma following a natural disaster, the **Butterfly Hug** is a simple self-holding technique that supports nervous system regulation and emotional safety.

Read through it entirely before beginning. You may find it helpful to record yourself reading it aloud, then play it back to guide yourself through the experience.

The goal of this technique is to calm the nervous system. You can experience some wonderful effects with regular practice, which include befriending the body and even opening the heart.

So, let's begin.

- Take two deep breaths, as you feel your feet on the floor and your bottom on your seat. Let your shoulders drop.
- Cross your arms over your chest, with the middle finger of each hand just below the collarbone.
- Hook your thumbs together—in the middle.
- Try to keep your hands more upright, so they point towards the neck, rather than the upper arms, but don't strain.
- Now imagine a beautiful butterfly is resting on your chest and flapping its wings, as you begin to tap with me: L and R, L and R, L and R.
- Use a little pressure so you can feel your flesh give a bit under the touch.

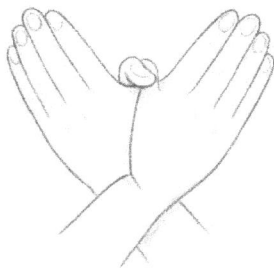

- Tap and breathe normally, or you can do deeper breaths—whatever feels good.
- Continue at whatever speed feels right for you, with eyes either closed or unfocused.

- If things pass through your mind and body, such as thoughts, images, sounds, feelings, or maybe physical sensations, just notice. Notice without the need to change, judge, or push anything away. You can pretend that what you're noticing is like clouds drifting by.
- We will be ending soon. When you're ready, let your hands be still and rest on your chest, and open your eyes.

I close my practice with a little self-hug, like a pat or rub on my arms. Of course, this is completely optional, and you may be curious to try it. If not, just put your hands down and take a deep cleansing breath in and out.

Finally, this is something you can share with your children if you have them. Kids really love it! Or even with the child inside of you, if that feels right.

The Butterfly Hug helps us connect with safety and self-soothing through the body. From that grounded place, we can also begin to connect through words.

Pause to Practice: A letter to myself

Sometimes our steadier selves need to remind the tender, uncertain parts of who we are when we forget. Writing a love note to yourself can help quiet the noise and make space for your inner wise elder to be heard.

Take some time to write or record a message to your future struggling self, directly from your healthiest/highest self—the inner healing intelligence we introduced earlier.

This message/letter can serve as a reminder to you at a future moment in time of who you are, at your essence. It can be as simple as 3 or 4 Post-it notes with some key messages that will remind your struggling self of who you truly are, it can be a full letter, or even a video to yourself. Whatever feels most congruent for you, lean into it and let your true nature/pilot light shine on your struggling self!

Keep this message close—it's a compass for the moments you forget your way. As you strengthen this inner relationship, notice how compassion starts to extend naturally outward. The next Waypoint explores this widening circle of connection—how our healing deepens through relationship, community, and spirit.

WAYPOINT 10: ACKNOWLEDGING OUR INTERCONNECTION

Earlier in this journey, we explored how community and secure relationships help regulate our nervous systems and build our resilience. Research echoes what wisdom traditions have always known: when we feel genuinely connected and supported, even the steepest of hills starts to feel more meaningful and more manageable (Davis et al., 2021). And it doesn't stop with people. Time in nature can have similar effects, calming the stress response and re-orienting us toward meaning.

There is a word for the kind of connection that can emerge in moments of shared meaning and vulnerability: *communitas*. Anthropologist Victor Turner used this term to describe a deep sense of belonging that arises when we move through liminal or transformative experiences together—when roles soften, defenses drop, and we feel held by something larger than ourselves (Turner, 1969). Communitas isn't just "community." It is what happens when separation dissolves and we sense, even briefly, the truth of our interconnectedness. Edith Turner describes communitas as a lived, embodied experience of shared vitality—something that can feel sacred, relational, and profoundly real (Turner, 2012).

This understanding of interconnection lies at the heart of the Roots to Thrive framework. Co-regulation—how our nervous systems settle in the presence of safety—extends beyond people to include the more-than-human world. Some Indigenous teachings refer to this wider kinship as *All My Relations*. In this view, land, water, plants, and animals are not a backdrop. They are kin and teachers, helping us return to trust and balance (Grizzlypaws, 2023). Reconnecting with plant relatives can also restore ancestral knowledge and deepen belonging to place (Joseph, 2023)

A Note on Spirituality and Religion: Spirituality and religion can overlap, but they aren't the same. Spirituality is about connection—to yourself, to others, to nature, to ancestors, and to something greater. It's grounded in relationship and lived experience, and it welcomes many beliefs. Religion usually refers to practices and teachings within a specific tradition. Both can support healing. A substantial body of research links spiritual and religious engagement—including prayer and relationship with the sacred—to improved well-being, resilience, and longevity (Koenig, 2012; VanderWeele, 2017; Chida et al., 2009). The kind of spirituality we explore here is open to everyone.

This perspective expands our understanding of relationship. Spirit may move through people, but also through all living things. Within this broader relational field, natural and spiritual allies are counted among us as compassionate witnesses and active participants in our healing.

When we attune to the web of life around us, we begin to sense that same steadiness and presence within ourselves. As Ladinsky's (2002) rendering of Hāfez reminds us:

The Centre of Everything

When you reach the centre of everything,
there is silence
the Beloved whispers,
"I am you."

At the core of interconnection lies the simple truth that we are not separate from the life moving around and through us. When we return to this centre, belonging shifts from an abstract concept to a felt reality.

Fuelling the Spirit Within

Spirituality means different things to different people. While often linked to religion, it's not the same. Drawing on the Māori-informed Just Therapy approach (Waldegrave et al., 1990), we can see spirituality as the sacred quality of relationship—between us, the land, our ancestors, and the unseen dimensions of life. In this sense, spirituality is deeply relational; it's the thread that connects us to ourselves, to one another, to the natural world, and to what feels greater than us.

Poet and philosopher Mark Nepo (2004) reminds us that each of us carries an unburdened place within—a spot of grace untouched by fear or striving. Across traditions, this inner essence has many names—the soul, the psyche, the atman, the qalb—but all point to the same source: an inner wellspring of wisdom and light.

Research shows this connection is not only poetic but practical. Spirituality can be a powerful source of hope and resilience, buffering stress and supporting our mental and physical health (Bożek & Nowak, 2020).

Reclaiming it often means turning from external achievement toward the wisdom that lives inside us. When we draw on spiritual resources—whether through meaning-making, ritual, or a sense of belonging—we often experience greater psychological well-being and healthier coping strategies.

Exploring spirituality helps us understand how we function as whole beings. Spirit, mind, and body each play unique yet connected roles in shaping our experience.

Anatomy of BEing: Channels between the ordinary & non-ordinary

To understand the whole self—mind, body, and spirit—we must recognize the different but connected ways we make sense of the world. At times, we move through ordinary awareness—thinking, planning, and relating. At other times, we access deeper states through meditation, prayer, or reflection, tapping into intuition and inner knowing.

- **Spirit** can be seen as a central flame—a conduit to the sacred and non-ordinary, guiding intuition, insight, and connection to something greater than the self.
- **Mind** serves as the meaning-making system, interpreting experience through thought and emotion.
- **Body** anchors us in the present moment, translating sensation into awareness and providing a somatic bridge for regulation and intuition.

Together, these aspects, illustrated in **Figure 15**, form a triad that supports our healing and resilience (Sá, 2025).

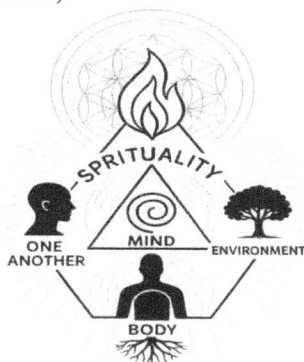

Figure 15. A central flame symbolizes Spirit—our link to the non-ordinary and sacred relationship. The radiating energy field reflects evidence-informed bioenergetics (Sá, 2025), while surrounding elements represent our connection to the living world. Together, Spirit, Mind, and Body form a triad that supports healing and resilience.

As we include these in our definition of what makes us whole, spirituality becomes a practical part of daily experience—a source of inspiration that supports our BEing and DOing.

Pause to Practice: Rooting and reaching

Adapted from a grounding practice shared by Helen Watler, lead somatic energy practitioner, whose teachings continue to guide our connection to body, breath, and earth.

We often use this grounding practice to prepare for psychedelic-assisted therapy sessions, helping participants *re-source* with nature—reminding us that support is always available, both within and around us.

This is a self-guided practice. As you read, pause briefly after each sentence or instruction. You may find it helpful to read it through once beforehand and adapt it into wording that feels natural, or to record yourself reading it and use the recording as you go.

Begin with a deep breath in through your nose and out through your mouth. If it feels comfortable, close your eyes or lower your gaze to turn inward.

Place your hands over your heart.

Imagine sending a taproot from the base of your spine down into the Earth.

With each breath, draw in its grounding, supportive energy.

Next, picture branches extending from the crown of your head into the sky.

With each breath, invite light energy to flow down into you.

Let these Earth and Sky energies meet and merge within you.

Breathe in loving-kindness... and breathe out loving-kindness.

Now, releasing your arms, imagine this energy expanding outward from your heart—radiating into the space around you.
Sense yourself receiving from the world in return—nourished by each breath and held by the land that's supporting you.

Let this flow continue, strengthening your sense of belonging and connection to something greater.

As you close the practice, let the sense of connection remain, and take a moment to notice how you feel.

Many find that connecting to the earth in this way supports steadiness and grounding, while connecting to the sky supports openness and expansion. Together, they offer a simple reminder: you are held by something beneath you and something beyond you—and you can draw on both as sources of support.

From this grounded openness—from the earth beneath you and the sky above—you may notice an inner steadiness that's already here. For some, this inner presence is experienced as Spirit or a connection to something greater. For others, it may feel like a steady part of the self that knows how to meet challenge and change.

Circling back to the attachment literature introduced in earlier Waypoints, practices like this can help expand attachment beyond human relationships. When we build a felt sense of connection with the natural world, we're also expanding our community of support—strengthening belonging and helping us feel held. Over time, that can grow a steadier sense of security and resilience, especially in times of uncertainty or change.

When we feel supported by what's around us, it becomes easier to notice what Elder Geraldine Manson calls our *pilot light*—the steady spark inside that stays with us through difficult times. It's our inner source of wisdom and energy, always present whether or not we think of it in spiritual terms.

104

Living from this state of BEing means we are trusting our inner wisdom—our pilot light—to guide our choices. As we learn to recognize and trust this inner signal—often felt as intuition—we gain a deeper sense of alignment with ourselves and the world around us. This signal is quiet but dependable. It helps us tune out the noise of the world, so we can reconnect with what truly matters to us. Over time, our actions (DOing) begin to flow more naturally from this grounded place of BEing. We stop striving to prove ourselves and start living in alignment with our values, desires, and purpose.

As we integrate these practices into daily life, a deeper rhythm begins to emerge—one that connects intention, action, and meaning. Across cultures and traditions, this connection has often been nurtured through *faith* and *ritual*—not as doctrines or obligations, but as living practices that help us remember what matters most.

In this way, faith—when practiced, not just believed—becomes a compass. It helps us orient toward meaning, even when the path ahead isn't clear. Rituals then become the expression of that **faith.** They are the bridges between our inner truth and the outer world—helping us stay congruent with what matters most and reinforcing our sense of coherence: the feeling that life is understandable, manageable, and meaningful.

Faith as Living Practice: Spiritual anchoring as a resilience factor

Faith is a habit of mind—a quiet compass guiding our path through uncertainty.

Faith, in the context of healing, is more than belief in something unseen—it's a way of living that reflects what matters most. It's an embodied orientation toward meaning, purpose, and trust, especially within uncertain times.

When lived out through prayer, meditation, reflection, or community, faith becomes a steadying force. It grounds us, connects us, and helps us meet life's challenges with greater confidence and equanimity.

Spiritual engagement supports both emotional and physical health. People who practice faith regularly tend to experience lower levels of anxiety and depression, stronger social support, and greater resilience. These practices are also associated with longer life and overall well-being (Long et al., 2024).

Faith has its greatest impact when it's lived out—when beliefs are expressed through meaningful action. These actions might look like prayer and meditation—both of which regulate the nervous system, calm stress responses, and restore balance in the body (DeSteno et al., 2019). Community amplifies these effects, reminding us that we belong, even when life feels uncertain.

Faith can be a bridge to resilience. It can widen our sense of support and secure connection—not only with people, but also with nature, ancestors, and the sacred (Winter & Granqvist, 2023). This kind of connection can strengthen a felt sense of safety and belonging, helping us recover and grow through adversity.

Faith can also support a sense of coherence—experiencing life as more understandable, manageable, and meaningful (Antonovsky, 1987)—and religious or spiritual engagement has been shown to strengthen coherence by helping people make meaning of hardship (Jeserich et al., 2023). From this view, resilience is not only an individual trait; it's also relational and systemic, shaped by the networks and environments that hold us (Mittelmark, 2021). Faith then becomes more than what we believe—it becomes a relational source of steadiness, courage, and trust.

Faith further nurtures congruence, the alignment between our inner experience and outer expression (Rogers, 1959). While this alignment often develops in human relationships, it can also emerge through spiritual attachment—to nature, ancestors, or a benevolent presence (Winter & Granqvist, 2023). When faith is embodied, it naturally seeks expression. The connection we feel within moves outward—through movement, rhythm, and intention—and this is where **ritual** begins.

Ritual: Bridging DOing and BEing

For many of us in contemporary secular settings, the term ritual can feel unfamiliar and intimidating. As a beloved member of our team and mentor in ceremony and ritual, Rev. Dr. Gail Peekeekoot observes,

> We have, more and more, become passive observers in our society, rather than active participants. Where we once engaged in ritual and ceremony both individually and in community, we now regard them more as forms of entertainment rather than instruments of transformation—making and marking change. This has led to a loss of deeper meaning. …At the same time, increased use of tech devices has led us to become more isolated—observing rather than engaging in social life. *(personal communication, December 5, 2025)*

By ritual, we mean simple, intentional actions we repeat because they help us remember what truly matters and keep us connected—to ourselves, to each other, and to something greater than us. Scholars describe ritual as patterned, symbolic action—a "set-apart" pocket of time or space where ordinary actions take on extra meaning (Bell, 1992; Durkheim, 1912; Tambiah, 1979; Humphrey & Laidlaw, 1994; Beumer, 2020).

Many rituals begin with something small and tangible: a touchstone we can see, hold, or repeat—a stone in our pocket, the simple act of lighting a candle before we begin, a hand to the heart, a phrase we whisper, or a small intentional space we pass by each day. Like carrying a seed, these cues help us remember our pillars of strength and return us to what matters when stress pulls us off course. The power is not in the object itself, but in the relationship we build with it and the intention it helps us embody (Grimes, 2000).

106

Rituals aren't just routines. They are meaningful actions that bring rhythm and structure to daily life. They help us pause, listen, and act from a place of authenticity and presence. Because our nervous system learns through repetition, even very brief rituals can become familiar pathways back to safety, regulation, and a sense of agency (Hobson et al., 2018).

Intentional rituals support a shift from reactive to restorative. They can nourish the spirit, calm stress responses, balance emotions, and reinforce helpful neural pathways—making them powerful tools for resilience and integration. Over time, these practices become sustaining anchors: habits that help us live our values in everyday life, turning what matters most into simple, intentional actions. These practices create rhythm and connection, building a resilient foundation to stand on. As O'Donohue (2002) reminds us, we are wise to recognize the moments in our lives that would benefit from being "clothed in ritual."

Pause to Practice: Meaningful objects as benefactors
by Julia Sheffield, RTT Senior Facilitator

A *benefactor* is someone or something that offers help or advantage—a source of support. In many spiritual lineages, creating and tending a benefactor space can be a form of ritual that is kept alive through consistent care—refreshing it, cleaning it, and returning to it—so it continues to function as a reliable anchor in day-to-day life.

As we create and care for an intentional space, we associate that space with feelings of calm and safety. In time, simply seeing or thinking about that space can cue those same feelings (Orbell & Verplanken, 2020; Smith & Vela, 2001).

Consider setting up an intentional spot in your home with items that comfort you or remind you of your strengths—photos of loved ones, a cherished pet, spiritual symbols, or even public figures who inspire you. Place it somewhere you'll see every day and tend to it regularly, as consistency is a key part of building the benefits described above. With intention, these benefactors become allies we can lean on when life feels heavy. They remind us that we are connected and that we don't have to carry our burdens alone.

Bringing it Altogether: A resilience ecosystem

These elements form a resilience ecosystem—a living network that weaves together faith, attachment, coherence, and ritual into an integrated whole. Faith-based attachment widens our circle of unconditional positive regard, extending secure connection beyond human relationships to include the natural world, our ancestors, and what we experience as sacred. This broader sense of belonging helps us feel seen, held, and supported—especially in moments of vulnerability. From this grounded place of being held, secure attachment has room to grow. It creates the safety we need to live in congruence—where our inner truth and outer expression align. When we feel accepted by something greater than ourselves, congruence becomes possible, allowing us to act with integrity.

Rituals help anchor this alignment. In a world full of uncertainty, rituals offer rhythm, predictability, and a sense of agency—simple ways to return to what we can influence. They bridge BEing with DOing, helping us embody our values and strengthening our sense that, even in uncertainty, things can still be manageable and meaningful (sense of coherence). More than practices, rituals become tangible expressions of faith—reminders of our pillars of strength and our place within the larger unfolding.

Together, these elements prepare the ground for Generativity—the process of letting meaningful actions take root and shape our habits, our choices, and the path we walk forward.

WAYPOINT 11: GENERATIVITY—OUR WAY FORWARD

As we build on the practices of faith and ritual introduced earlier, this Waypoint asks us to notice how meaningful actions start to settle in—shaping our habits, our choices, and ultimately, our way of BEing and DOing. What once required effort may now feel more natural. This is *integration*: the moment when what we've learned becomes something we embody.

Habits, like roots, take time to grow. On average, it takes about 59 to 66 days for a new habit to become automatic (Lally et al., 2010). Each time we return to a practice that feels meaningful, we reinforce the pathways that support it. With repetition, these practices begin to become part of a rhythm that connects and sustains us.

As neuroscience shows, the part of our brain that helps us stay aligned with our values—the anterior cingulate cortex—gets stronger with practice. This means that even when something feels awkward at first, it can become second nature over time (Touroutoglou et al., 2020).

This is what generativity is all about—not just continuing the work, but letting it become part of how we live. It's less about collecting new tools and more about recognizing what's already working for us.

Instead of reaching for more, this waypoint reminds us to pause and take stock. To notice who we've become, or perhaps who we've come home to. To keep nourishing our BEing with practices that feel natural and true. And to let our DOing flow from that place—not as proof of worth, but as an offering to ourselves and the world.

Generativity is what emerges when we live from the inside out—when our values, actions, and ways of being come into alignment. Over time, this sense of coherence becomes our resilience: a trust in the flow of life and in our capacity to meet what arises. Through community, intention, and steady practice, we strengthen the roots that keep us grounded and the branches that help us grow toward what feels meaningful.

Generativity
by Wes Taylor, Facilitator and Senior Trainer

In the process of this journey, we've extended our roots, feeling into the nurturing soil that holds us. We need our roots to gather life energy from source—to help us remember the essence of who we are. These roots hold us steady in the storms. Strong winds carry the old away, clearing space to make way for something new.

How do we keep alive these profound experiences of unconditional positive regard, belonging in community, deep spiritual cleansing and awakening, and inspirations we've embodied along the way? This is the question of sustainability—or generativity.

To do this, we make it a Way of Life: live the essence of who I am as best I can and do my best to use the various practices that I have learned to nourish my BEing. It's DOing to support BEing.

Don't try to fill your pockets in this last part of the journey or look for tools you haven't yet picked up. Instead, take a moment to review who you've become along the way.

What have you come to know and experience as true about you? I'm not speaking of new positive beliefs, as beliefs are mental structures to which we cling to navigate in this world of form. Necessary, yes—but deeply insufficient for a fully lived life.

Replacing negative beliefs with positive ones is helpful, but if we stay mired in mental and abstract thinking, we risk staying disconnected from our true nature. I'm speaking of the direct experience that happens before belief—the deep peace that you have touched during these weeks, the truth that you do matter, you do belong, you're inextricably part of all that is…the truth that your essence is whole, undamaged, and pure.

These are not concepts but rather *felt experiences* that you have tasted, passed through, or now recognize. Return to these experienced, felt truths in whatever ways have worked for the past eleven weeks—those now-familiar ways of placing your attention on your sensations, your breath, tapping, etc.

It's good to do a deep dive into our healing and growth periodically. You have just had one. And just like going to the dentist, having a deep cleaning once every six months (or twelve months in my case, as I really don't like going to the dentist) will not keep your teeth healthy if you don't tend to them daily.

It must become a way of life—effortless, unquestioned, habit. *What are those effortless habits of awareness, grounding, opening your heart in self-compassion, and alignment with your essence that you have already established?* Keep them up. Those are your practices.

Integration is like learning a dance—you'll miss steps sometimes, but the music is still playing. Just keep coming back to the rhythm.

Your way of life is all about practice—RTT has offered many examples. As the common phrase goes, neurons and neural networks that fire together, wire together—they get stronger. This is the neurobiology behind the value of practice.

So please remember we are always practicing something—we are always strengthening some neural network or other.

110

My friend and teacher of Living Compassion, Robert Gonzales, once shared a question that stopped him in his tracks: *"What are you practicing—what are you 'meditating'—in each moment?"* He realized we're always focused on something. Life is a kind of meditation. When we run on autopilot—following old habits of thought and action—we often end up somewhere we didn't choose. But when we bring awareness to what we're giving our attention to, we can shift from judgment and evaluation toward what's more true and life-giving underneath. I watched Robert do this in real time: noticing the mind's reflex to appraise, then turning toward deeper needs—what he sometimes called life energy. He was one of the most awake people I've known.

We can't talk about sustainability without talking about community. We aren't meant to do this alone. Like trees in a forest, we survive through connection—roots and mycelial networks that share nutrients when needed and even signal danger so others can protect themselves. In hard seasons, we lean on each other; in easier seasons, we give freely. This isn't extra. It's part of how resilience works.

Bottom line:

They need each other.
We need each other.

The Anglo-Irish poet and philosopher David Whyte (2015), whose work bridges Celtic mythology and contemplative practice, invites us to see relationship as a sacred act of witnessing. He writes that true friendship isn't about improvement or fixing, but about presence—the mutual recognition and witnessing of each other's essence. In this view, to be seen and to see another with honesty and compassion becomes a form of belonging in itself—a medicine for isolation, and a mirror of the wholeness we all share.

So, double down on those communities or relationships where witnessing is happening. Ask yourself: *What's one thing I can contribute to cultivate or deepen my community?* And if those spaces don't yet exist for you, seek out—or create—communities where witnessing, grounded in unconditional positive regard, is woven into their very fabric.

Now, here's the difficult news about RTT: it's a resilience program—no cures promised.

For those of you who have had curative, healing experiences, you have been touched by grace and can trust that true healing does happen.

At the same time, we are all going to get smacked in the face with the struggles and challenges that are part of life. The best paradoxical practice that I know is to embrace the down times and know they will pass. They are unavoidable.

They are not evidence of your failure nor of the permanent return of your demons. They only confirm your humanness—and they are important messengers in this way.

At first, it takes a supported growth process to be able to tolerate anguish and despair. Bit by bit, you have been learning to sit with uncomfortable emotions as your window of tolerance for suffering expands.

As you continue healing, you can begin to accept that these episodes happen and cease fighting when they visit. Then, over time, see if you can cultivate a sense of welcome—find that place in your essence that's undisturbed by pain, fear, shame, or despair.

Welcome the painful experience into your being and allow it to move through you and leave its wake. Allow yourself to be changed, reformed, reborn into each new moment.

It's not the waves of life themselves, but our clinging to rigid identities—our resistance to what's unfolding—that deepens our suffering.

As the great Sufi poet Hāfez reminds us through the interpretive lens of Daniel Ladinsky (1999):

Don't Surrender your Loneliness

Don't surrender your loneliness
So quickly.
Let it cut more deep.
Let it ferment and season you
As few human
Or even divine ingredients can.
Something missing in my heart tonight
Has made my eyes so soft,
My voice
So tender,
My need of God
Absolutely
Clear.
— *Hāfez, interpreted by Daniel Ladinsky (1999)*

When we learn to lean into challenges—trusting our pillars of strength and the tools that remind our body it's going to be okay—we build confidence and courage. Like weight training, the hardest reps strengthen us the most. Using these tools when you least want to builds our resilience in powerful ways.

These experiences teach us to trust both the benefits and our capacity to navigate hard times. And remember, practicing when life feels smooth helps turn these tools into habits you can rely on when things get tough.

We cannot and will not stay in harmony, in perfect self-connection day in and day out. Success can't be defined by always staying 'strong'. A better standard is this: *how quickly do I notice I'm struggling, and can I return to practices that rekindle my pilot light?* "Good enough" is the goal here—and self-compassion matters as much as the speed of recovery. When we can identify when we're struggling and respond with self-compassion, we will have greater resilience in the face of adversity (Park et al., 2024).

Don't try to do it all at once. Choose one or two practices to focus on. Test them—let them prove their value or eliminate them if they don't fit. Once those practices feel natural and have become part of your way of life, then consider adding others. The most effective tools are the ones you *actually* use.

Set and setting are important and aren't just terms for psychedelic medicine (explored further in the appendices)—they're about where you are and how you are. Set is your inner state: your mindset, intentions, and emotional tone. Setting is your outer environment: the people, spaces, and conditions around you. Both shape how you experience life.

So, cultivate your inner landscape with mantras, calling statements, self-regulation practices, and open-hearted intentions. And design your outer environment with care—because research shows that those who surround us profoundly shape who we become; context activates patterns of thought, emotion, and behavior (Van Der Gaag et al., 2025). Together, your mindset and your setting form the architecture of your becoming.

Ask yourself: *What environments are you hanging out in? Do they nourish you? Are you walking intentionally on the earth, spending time touching moss and smelling the forests? Are you surrounding yourself with relationships that are nurturing and nourishing?*

We naturally mirror the people we spend the most time with. Our deeply social brains and interconnected neural networks shape how we think, feel, and experience life. Because of this profound influence, it's essential to design your relational environment with intention—rather than leaving it to chance.

We are awash in the reminders to engage in deliberate gratitude these days. That's a powerful teaching. I want to underscore this guidance: not only with celebrating—consciously attending to/appreciating that which enriches life and dwelling in that experience for a while—but also with mourning. The painful aspects of life hold gifts within them. Try not to rush past hard feelings by immediately "doing a tool" (tapping, 4-7-8 breathing, etc.) and calling it self-connection. Sometimes connection starts with staying present.

Feel the pain, breathe space around it, and hold it within compassion. When you hold it (yourself) with compassion and care, you can find the essence of the pain. Then you can come to see it as something cherished, deeply valued that you have lost contact with. What a beautiful thing to hurt for!

We only grieve for those qualities that are precious and held dear in our hearts. In this way, celebration and mourning are opposite sides of a single coin—a coin of incomparable value and meaning.

For me, this way of life is about living in surrender—surrendering to the natural flow of life. Discovering and releasing those blocks and eddies in which I get stuck, in order to more fully re-enter the life-stream. Father Thomas Keating, Trappist Monk and teacher of Centring Prayer (a Christian version of meditation) said that we have but one action—one aspect of effort necessary for a spiritual way of life, and that is to 'consent to the presence and activity of [the divine].' *Just consent.*

This way of life is expressed beautifully in teachings from fellow traveller Jalāl ad-Dīn Muhammad Rūmī. The piece below is an interpretive rendering of his original Persian poetry, intended to carry its contemplative spirit into contemporary English. These words invite us inward—into stillness, listening, and the quiet consent that allows the next step of becoming to unfold.

Be Silent

Be still, be silent, silence reigns before life and beyond death.
You cry, begging for generous ones to help;
finally hear, without divine grace we are lost – we are nothing.

So, become still, silent… stop every effort.

When the soul cries on its own, a sea of mercy answers.

There is no centre in the heart of the Infinite;
from this emptiness, being is born.

Be silent, be silent…
realizing you are not a prophet, be of the community and listen,
so go, be silent.

Any drop of insight you carry will rejoin the sea of wisdom there.

Inspired by themes from Rumi's Masnavi-ye Ma'navi. This piece is an interpretive rendering by Wes Taylor, created with the support of AI translation tools, to evoke the spirit and contemplative tone of the original Persian poetry in contemporary English.

Having glimpsed the beauty that emerges through surrender, we are reminded that thriving requires not only inspiration but also intentional clearing. To sustain our thriving roots, we must gently remove or release what obstructs them—old patterns, dense emotions, and rigid attachments that keep us stuck. This next section invites us into that process.

Unblocking the Path to Thriving: Clearing out the sticky bits

We all feel stuck sometimes. It might show up as heaviness in the body, looping thoughts, or emotions that seem to linger longer than we'd like—grief, anger, shame, fear. These aren't signs that something is wrong with you. They're signs that something inside is asking to be felt, witnessed, and when it's ready, released.

Stuckness isn't a flaw—it's the body's way of holding onto what hasn't yet had the chance to be metabolized. Often, these emotions were too overwhelming to feel at the time they first arose. So, they stayed tucked away, waiting for a moment when we feel safe enough to meet them.

It's okay to feel whatever we're feeling. Where emotions get stuck is when they run into our judgment of them. They don't need to be judged—they're simply trying to show us something important, even when they're uncomfortable. All emotions are part of being human. But when we judge them or dwell too long in the heavier ones—like resentment, guilt, or despair—they can cloud our perspective and weigh down our spirit. Over time, this can affect not just our emotional well-being, but our physical and spiritual health too.

Many healing traditions—Indigenous, Ayurvedic, and Chinese medicine— have long recognized that emotional and energetic imbalances can affect our health. Western science is beginning to reflect this too; for example, research shows that heavy emotional states like chronic anger can place stress on the heart (McCraty, 2016). *The hopeful part?* Difficult emotions can shift. Feelings such as gratitude, curiosity, forgiveness, or even a bit of humour carry lighter, more open energy. They help us move from protection into connection— from effort into ease. This is the heart of *emotional transmutation*: meeting what we feel, understanding the message it carries, and allowing it to change us.

Transmutation isn't about pretending to be positive. It's about giving ourselves room to heal—learning to trust emotions as signals and leaning on the supports that help us move with life rather than against it. These more open emotional states become tools—what we've called *significant actions*—those intentional actions that sustain our agency, helping us meet life with more choice and confidence.

Transmuting *Stuckness* with Gratitude

Sometimes, when we feel stuck in pain or overwhelm, it can be hard to see what's still good. Gratitude doesn't erase the hard stuff—but it helps us remember what's still here, still holding us. It's a way to shift our emotional state, not by bypassing what hurts, but by making space for what heals.

Gratitude shifts our emotional trajectory by focusing on what we have, rather than what we lack. This shift isn't just a change in thinking—it's a change in energy. It can transmute the heaviness of suffering into something more spacious and empowering.

How grateful we feel often depends on our expectations and our sense of worthiness. When we receive more than we expect or believe we deserve, gratitude naturally arises. And the more grateful we feel, the more joy and contentment we experience (Watkins et al., 2018).

Research shows that gratitude improves overall well-being and happiness (Wood & Maltby, 2009), enhances sleep (Wood et al., 2009), reduces stress (Solberg & Segerstrom, 2006), deepens relationship satisfaction, and strengthens spiritual connection (Bartlett & DeSteno, 2006). Recent findings also show that when paired with emotional regulation, gratitude significantly boosts body compassion and health-related intentions—further reinforcing its role in healing and resilience (Dennis & Ogden, 2025).

It's important to remember that gratitude isn't a tool for avoiding difficult emotions. Healing requires us to feel what arises. Suppressed emotions remain stuck in the body until they are acknowledged and processed. Gratitude helps us hold space for those emotions—not to bypass them, but to meet them with more openness.

To feel grateful, we put our attention on the positive aspects of life. This means noticing the gifts we often overlook or take for granted. By immersing ourselves in gratitude, we interrupt the powerlessness that can arise from entitlement or victimhood. Gratitude isn't about pretending everything's fine—it's about noticing what's still good, even when things are hard. From this empowered state, we can face discomfort with greater confidence.

Gratitude helps reorient our nervous system away from fear and toward regulation and connection. It boosts our capacity to navigate life's challenges and feel the emotions that need to be felt. In this way, *gratitude becomes a bridge—not a bypass*—helping us transmute suffering into understanding.

And from this bridge, something begins to move outward. When gratitude is consistently felt—not just as a fleeting emotion but as a way of being—it begins to shape how we relate to others. Research shows that people who regularly experience gratitude are more likely to engage in acts of kindness and support, suggesting that service is not a separate act but a natural extension of gratitude itself (Zhu et al., 2024).

Gratitude doesn't just help us feel better—it helps us show up better. It becomes a quiet force that nourishes connection, reinforces meaning, and invites us to participate in the healing of others as part of our own.

Yet this flow of gratitude into service can feel distant when we're in the depths of pain. When hardship clouds our view, gratitude becomes more complex—less about what we offer, and more about how we begin to see. This brings us to an important question…

How Can I Have Gratitude for Hardship?

Gratitude becomes more complex when we're faced with pain, loss, or trauma. It's not about pretending everything is okay—it's about discovering the healing, wisdom, or gifts that may have emerged through the struggle. Sometimes, the lessons come wrapped in difficulty, and it's okay if we're not ready to appreciate them right away.

If it's hard to see the gift in a painful experience, start with compassion. Meet the part of yourself still holding that pain with kindness. You might say, *that was awful. I'll never let that happen again.* That protective instinct, once necessary for survival, can evolve into wisdom. And that wisdom is something we can be grateful for.

The teachings of Robert Gonzales, from his Living Compassion curriculum, make the distinction of the *pain of the unmet need* as different from the *beauty of the need* itself (personal communication with Wes Taylor, 2009). If we have lost someone we love, there is certainly grief and ache in that loss. Simultaneously, love itself lives strongly at the heart of that pain and can be accessible to us as we grieve and heal. This living energy of love (or of any universal need) is what makes life worth living. As one of our RTT nurses, Jo Hall, has says, *"what a beautiful thing to hurt for!"* We only hurt or ache about those experiences that we value. In this way, gratitude can be found even in hardship. This is not a suggestion to avoid the pain, but to allow the beauty beneath it to emerge naturally on the healing path.

Gratitude isn't just a concept—it's a vibrational state that helps us transform painful memories. But it's important to be honest with ourselves. If we're only going through the motions, trying to 'think positive' without feeling the truth of our experience, we risk spiritual bypassing. Real healing asks us to bring our whole selves to the process—mind, body, and spirit. We need to feel the pain of the unmet need fully. If you notice a block, it's okay to seek support. Talking things out, somatic practices, or other healing modalities can help you move through what feels stuck.

When we stay focused on what's been lost, we can miss what's trying to grow. Gratitude for hardship doesn't mean condoning what happened—it means reclaiming our power to grow from it. It's about shifting our gaze from what fell away (the particular form) to what's important within the experience (the essence)—because we're grounded in what's real and true right now. When we meet the moment with understanding, purpose, and confidence—the core elements of sense of coherence—new possibilities can emerge. Research supports this connection: when we're stuck in old patterns of thinking, it becomes harder to recognize and nurture fresh opportunities (Wang et al., 2023). Gratitude helps break that cycle by shifting our focus from what's gone to what's emerging. It's a way of saying, *I've been through something hard, and I'm still here. And from here, I can grow.*

To experience this shift directly, we'll pause for a brief practice to support transmuting with gratitude.

Pause to Practice: Transmuting with gratitude

Gratitude isn't just something we think—it's something we feel in our bodies, like warmth spreading through the chest when we remember what's still good. Along with the felt sense, our biology shifts too. When we engage with it authentically, our brains release dopamine, a feel-good chemical that supports joy and reinforces habits that nourish our well-being. But for gratitude to truly work its magic, it must be inspired, not forced. If we're just going through the motions, the emotional shift won't land.

A few notes before we begin: If gratitude feels out of reach, that's okay. Begin with compassion. Gratitude often follows—not as a demand, but as an arrival.

This list is intentionally broad—not meant to be completed all at once. Think of it as a menu, not a checklist. Let your body and heart guide you toward what feels meaningful. You might return to this list over time, noticing which practices call to you in different seasons of life.

Gratitude Practices (Choose 1–2 to explore):

- Recall one thing you're grateful for today. Let it anchor you when challenges arise.
- Name one quality or strength you appreciate in yourself.
- When offered a compliment, receive it with a simple thank you.
- When you feel inadequate, pause to remember your shared humanity. Gratitude for yourself begins with recognizing that we all carry both strengths and struggles.
- Express gratitude creatively—beyond thank you.
- Look beneath behaviours to the wounds they protect. Gratitude begins with compassion for the parts of you that kept you safe.
- When longing arises, invite gratitude to join you. Let it remind you how far you've come and all that you already have.
- Savour life's pleasures—stretch out the moments that bring joy.
- Write a note of gratitude to someone—or to yourself.
- Reflect on your mortality. Let it deepen your appreciation for those around you.
- Remember your connectedness. Gratitude grows when we recognize that even small acts contribute to something greater.
- Smile softly as you move through your day. Let it be an expression of gratitude—for yourself, for others, for the moment. Replace sorry with thank you—e.g., Thanks for your patience.
- When behind on a task, celebrate what you've already accomplished.

- Say no when your body signals a boundary. Gratitude for your own needs begins with honouring them.
- Do something you desire—just because you're grateful for yourself. Let it be a celebration of your worth.

Take a moment to notice how each of the practices felt in your body as you read them.

- Which 1–2 practices feel most meaningful or doable for you right now?
- When during your day might you naturally make space for a gratitude practice—morning coffee, a walk, or before bed?
- What challenges tend to pull you off centre? Is there a practice that might help you stay grounded in those moments?
- How might you remind yourself to engage in the practice—a sticky note, a phone reminder, a visual cue?

Gratitude helps us soften the edges of our experience—transforming what feels heavy into something more spacious and workable. Yet sometimes, what we need isn't just tenderness, but a spark of levity. This is where **humour** becomes a powerful ally.

Comic Relief for the Soul

Like gratitude, humour loosens the knots of rigidity, but it does so with playful energy that reminds us not to take ourselves—or life's inevitable challenges—too seriously.

By bringing lightness to challenging situations, it helps release rigid thought patterns and restore perspective. Because stress is often rooted in perception, humour can reduce its intensity, offering a less threatening frame (León-Pérez et al., 2021).

Beyond its cognitive benefits, humour also has a positive psychophysiological impact. Joy and laughter can enrich social connections, improve emotional regulation, and support focus and clarity (Savage et al., 2017).

However, discernment is key. Humour can also be used to deflect discomfort or communicate indirectly, which may erode trust or connection. When using humour, consider: *Is this helping me move toward connection, or away from it?*

Humour, like gratitude, shows us that even in difficulty, light can still get in. It eases fear and brings us back to joy—the energy that fuels our creativity, connection, and courage. When we let joy in, we naturally open the door to *play*.

Playing Our Way Back Home

Play has a way of bringing us home to ourselves. It reminds us of what it feels like to be safe enough to soften and free enough to simply be who we are.

Like humour, play helps us loosen up and reconnect with our own aliveness. And when we've been living in survival mode—always bracing, always scanning—it makes perfect sense that play feels distant. That isn't a personal flaw. It's your nervous system doing exactly what it learned to do to keep you safe. *The hopeful part?* We don't need to *learn* how to play. We already know. It's in us. We just need the right conditions to remember.

And even though we often associate play with children, it matters just as much in adulthood. Research shows that play supports emotional well-being and resilience, strengthening emotional intelligence and positive emotional states while offering healthier pathways for regulating stress (Ho, 2022). Adults who engage in play also tend to experience greater well-being and more satisfying relationships, suggesting that playfulness continues to support healthy connection throughout life (Proyer, 2014).

From a neuroscience perspective, play isn't optional—it's foundational. It's considered an evolutionarily conserved emotional system that supports social bonding and emotional development across the lifespan (Panksepp & Biven, 2012). In therapeutic settings, play-based approaches help create enough safety and openness for people to explore difficult material while staying connected and supported (Ray, 2019). Taken together, the science reinforces what many of us feel intuitively: play helps us think more flexibly and supports the nervous system in finding its way back to balance.

So, if you catch yourself giggling at a silly meme, doodling in the margins of your notes, or dancing around your kitchen while you make dinner—celebrate it. These moments aren't distractions. They're signs that your body is starting to feel safe enough to soften again. It's joy knocking on the door—and maybe, for the first time in a long while, you're ready to crack it open. Not forever. Not all at once. Just long enough to remember what home feels like.

WAYPOINT 12: LIVING A CALLING—OUR NORTH STAR

Living your calling feels like breathing easy—when what you do finally matches who you are inside.

Living our calling isn't just about passion—it's about alignment, letting who we are flow naturally into what we do. At its heart is integrity—the feeling of being whole and steady when our values, actions, and way of being move together in harmony.

In that spaciousness, the deeper longings of the heart can finally be heard. What once felt like striving becomes listening—attuning to the call that arises not from fear or duty, but from meaning and purpose.

This final Waypoint invites us to focus on the horizon—to orient by the North Star that has been present all along. Like a lighthouse, it lights the path ahead through fog and uncertainty. Here, the journey comes full circle: we integrate what we've learned, clarify what truly matters, and step into a life shaped by authenticity, grace, and a deep sense of meaning and confidence in our capacity to meet what comes.

This theme of returning to inner clarity is echoed in one of the earliest known collections of women's writing, the *Therīgāthā*. It captures the stillness and peace found when we reconnect with our own inner light:

> Tranquil, released, with mind like a clear lake,
> I saw within myself the source of peace.
> — trans. B. Sujato *(c. 6th–3rd century BCE)*

This inner steadiness—what these early teachers described as peace—mirrors what contemporary research identifies as living in accordance with our calling. When our actions flow from clarity and purpose, we experience greater harmony between our inner and outer life.

Research supports this view, showing that living our calling is associated with greater satisfaction, well-being, and engagement—especially when we can identify and embody our purpose (Ehrhardt & Ensher, 2021).

The North Star stays fixed in the night sky while other stars move around it, serving as a steady guide for those navigating the unknown. In the same way, we each carry an inner North Star—a light that helps us find our way back to what matters most.

When we lose sight of that inner light, it's easy to feel unmoored or unsure where to start. Sometimes this shows up as hesitation or avoidance—what we often call procrastination. But procrastination isn't just poor time management; it's often a signal that something deeper needs care. It can point to lost inspiration, a lack of choice, or feeling disconnected from meaning.

Research reminds us that procrastination tends to grow in controlling environments and ease when autonomy is supported (Codina et al., 2018). When our basic needs for choice and competence are frustrated, avoidance is more likely (Zhang et al., 2024). In this way, procrastination can be a teacher— inviting us to notice where inspiration, choice, or agency might need to be restored.

When we calm the noise in the inner and outer world, and learn to drop in and listen, we start to come into relationship with the call waiting beneath the surface. This inner calling isn't something we have to create—it's something we've carried all along.

Like the North Star, it's a steady light—always there as a patient presence and guide as we find our way home. The next practice helps give that light a voice: by creating a calling statement, it serves as a bridge between what feels true inside and how it's expressed in our daily lives.

Pause to Practice: Calling statement—a bridge to our North Star

Set aside 10-15 minutes where you won't be disturbed. Ask yourself these questions, and jot down your thoughts without overthinking:

- What makes me feel alive and energized?
- When do I feel most connected to myself and others?
- What do I deeply care about or feel called to contribute to the world?
- If I could dedicate myself to one thing that brings purpose and meaning, what would it be?

Identify Common Themes: Look at your answers and highlight key words or phrases that repeat or stand out. These could be emotions, values, passions, or specific actions.

Draft Your Calling Statement: Using the themes you identified, write a short and simple statement that reflects your personal calling. Focus on clarity and heart. It could be something like:

I am called to inspire creativity and connection in others.
My purpose is to support healing and growth in my community.
I strive to bring joy and understanding to those around me.

Read your statement out loud. *Does it feel true to you?* Revise as needed.

Keep your calling statement somewhere visible—on your desk, phone, or journal—so it can serve as a reminder of what matters most. Let it guide your choices and return to it often, updating it as you learn, grow, and evolve.

Living in Harmony with Our Calling

To live in harmony with our calling means embodying integrity—not as perfection, but as congruence between our values and actions. Integrity is an act of self-compassion—aligning what we believe with how we live is how we honour ourselves, even in the face of uncertainty. This becomes the integrity we stand on, and an inner compass that steers us toward choices that reflect our true nature. Living with integrity doesn't mean being flawless—it means returning to what matters, even when we stumble. *Good enough* isn't a compromise—it's a courageous way of being.

You might imagine you're calling as your heart's yearning—the spark that keeps your pilot light burning, the force that draws you forward with purpose. Integrity, then, is the bridge between that inner yearning and the actions you take in the world. To follow your calling with integrity means making decisions not out of fear, approval-seeking, or habit, but from a grounded understanding of who you are and what matters to you. Decisions are then informed by self-acceptance rather than self-doubt.

From the Ground Up: Tapping into what sustains us

Recognizing the resources we already have can strengthen our confidence in meeting life's challenges. This awareness can deepen our sense of coherence—that steady trust that we have what we need, and that we can find our way through.

As we grow into greater alignment with our calling, taking time to pause and reflect on what sustains us becomes part of the practice. Like a tree nourished by its roots, our resilience is strengthened by our inner resources, our connections, and the ways we offer ourselves to the world. The practice that follows supports us in identifying what's already here and the fruits that grow from that foundation.

Pause to Reflect: Root mapping—a practice in resourcefulness

Use the tree in **Figure 16** to reflect on your layers of support:

- **Roots:** *Your inner resources*—the qualities within you that keep you grounded and steady. These may include your values, strengths, passions, and the self-trust that helps you meet life as it is.
- **Foliage and branches:** *Your outer resources*—the people, practices, and environments that nourish you. These are the relationships and supports that remind you of your connections amid insecurity, and that help you return to centre amid uncertainty or self-doubt.
- **Fruits:** *The gifts you offer the world*—your contributions, expressions, and ways of being that touch others. These might include creativity, compassion, steadiness, leadership, humour, or care.

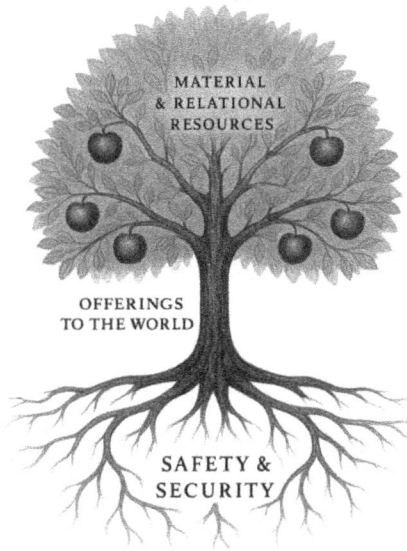

Figure 16. The tree illustrates our support system: roots as inner resources; branches as external supports; fruits as embodiments of offerings to the wider world.

Take a moment to pause and reflect on the roots, branches, and fruits that sustain you. These supports—both internal and external—help you return to centre and move forward with more clarity.

Optional: choose a touchstone. Choose a small, meaningful object that represents a seed you hope to nurture—perhaps a quality of self you're strengthening, or a relationship you're tending. Or choose an object that represents a *pillar of strength* you can rely on—something that reminds you of the strength of your root system. Keep it visible and accessible: by your bed, in your pocket, or in a place you pass often. When you notice stress showing up, let this be your cue to pause—hold it, take a slow breath, and remember your resources.

124

As you continue on your journey, let the rhythm of pausing, reflecting, and practicing guide your learning and growth. Consistent practice turns resilience into a lived experience—something you can return to, again and again.

A Final Blessing

May these words meet you where you are—reminding you of your inherent worth, your belonging, and the light that you alone can carry.

Awaken

to the rhythm of your breath,
to the stillness beneath the noise,
to the truth alive within you.

May awareness rise like morning light,
revealing not only what is,
but what longs to be.

May calm find you—
not as escape,
but as the steady beat of your own becoming.

May compassion guide your steps,
softening what has hardened,
holding what's still tender.

May you remember your birthright—
that singular thread entrusted to you,
an offering to our collective weaving,
already woven into the path you came here to walk.

This is your calling—
not something to earn,
but love made visible.

Blessings on your journey—
and on every step that returns you to your roots,
and to the safety of a world that can see
the beauty in all that you are,
and all you are becoming.

Appendix A: Describing Our Emotions

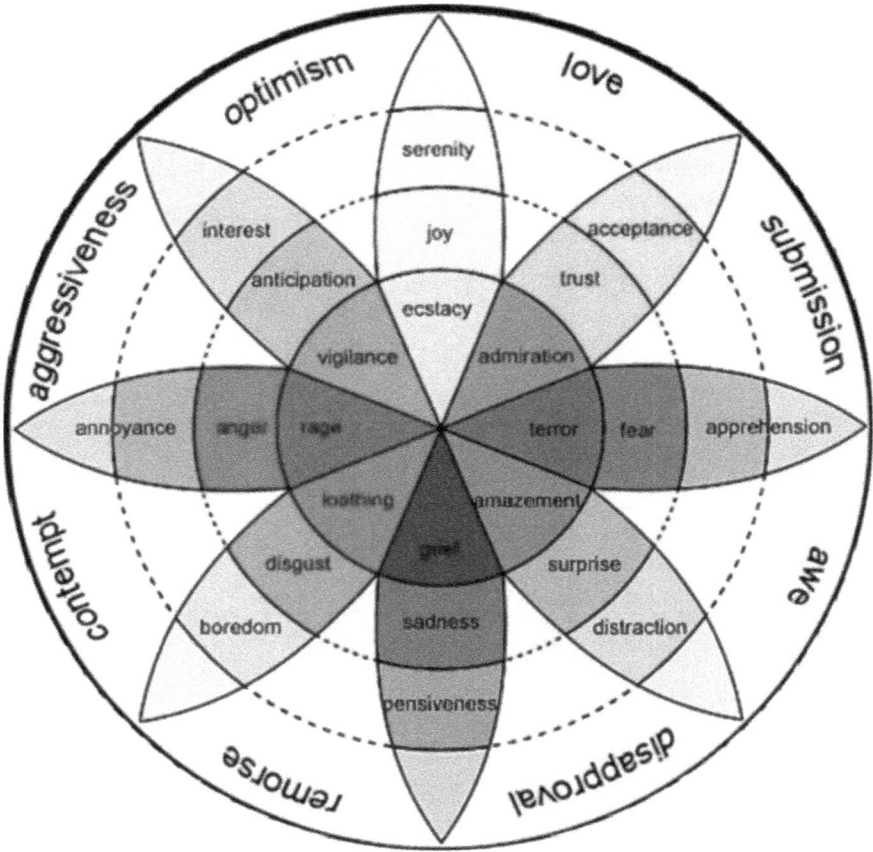

The "wheel of emotions" by Robert Plutchik, originally published in *American Scientist*, Vol. 89, No. 4 (July-August 2001), pp. 344-350. Used under the Creative Commons Attribution-ShareAlike 4.0 International (CC BY-SA 4.0) license.

The following appendices describe RTT medicine-assisted therapy as an optional adjunct to therapy and healing.

Even if you're reading from outside the program, you may find parallels with other therapeutic or community-based approaches.

These options are offered as invitations, not requirements. You can explore them if and when they feel right for you.

To learn more about RTT's medicine-assisted therapy, visit **www.rootstothrive.com**

Or email our navigator at **navigator@rootstothrive.com**
A referral form is required and can be accessed through the following QR code:

Appendix B: Psychedelic Medicines as Catalysts for Healing

Psychedelic-assisted therapy (PaT) is an additional offering in RTT. They act as catalysts for neuroplasticity, trauma resolution, and reconnection—supporting the inner healing intelligence and expanding the window of tolerance when traditional approaches may not suffice.

How Resilience Relates to PaT

PaT can support experiences such as increased insight (*awareness*), greater flexibility or space around intense emotions (*regulation*), expanded perspectives rooted in openness or care (*compassion*), and renewed clarity about what matters to us (*living with purpose and calling*). These experiences can be deeply meaningful—but they can also be disorganizing if the nervous system, relationships, or daily life lack sufficient support.

Resilience provides the ground that enables psychedelic experiences to be integrated—embodied and sustained—rather than overwhelming or fragmenting experience. It supports the capacity to:

- stay oriented during intense or unfamiliar states
- move through discomfort without collapsing or bypassing
- translate insight into sustainable changes in daily life
- return to relationship after vulnerability or rupture

From this perspective, resilience is not something psychedelics replace—it is something they can help build our resilience when the conditions are right. These medicines are one element within a broader ecosystem that includes preparation, relational safety, integration practices, and community support.

Everyone's path to well-being is unique. Some find healing through therapy, mindfulness, or self-regulation, while others may need physiological support to calm the nervous system and open access to their inner world. Seeking help to work with our biology isn't a weakness—it's wisdom born of self-understanding and shaped by both lived and ancestral experience. Research supports these insights, suggesting that psychedelics promote neuroplasticity, restore brain regions involved in connection, insight, and emotional resolution of trauma (Ly et al., 2018). By softening rigid patterns, they can reconnect us with a sense of aliveness, release stored pain, and open pathways for self-compassion.

Still, it's essential to remember that while psychedelics may help us remember our wholeness, they aren't *magic bullets*. Over time, we've come to understand that unconditional positive regard is the truest medicine—the treasure at the end of the rainbow. Psychedelics can remind us of this truth, but they remain allies, not the source of healing.

Non-ordinary States of Consciousness

Within RTT, psychedelic experiences often invite a shift from the ordinary state of consciousness into a non-ordinary one—a threshold moment where the ego softens, and habitual patterns loosen. In this expanded awareness, we may begin to see our stories with greater compassion and clarity. Past wounds are reframed not as personal failures, but as reflections of unmet pain—our own and others'. This widening of perspective fosters the grace and agency needed to relate to ourselves and the world with more love and understanding.

We use the term *non-ordinary* because it describes a crossing—a temporary opening where what was once hidden may surface. In this state, when the body's threat response quiets, we can safely meet emotions or memories that were too overwhelming to face before. From here, shame and regret can be transformed through the lens of unconditional positive regard. For those of us who have rarely experienced full acceptance, such moments can be profoundly healing—allowing parts of the self once hidden for safety to reemerge and integrate.

This experience of reconnection—of remembering that we belong to something greater—echoes truths held across spiritual and scientific traditions. As Einstein (1972) observed, our sense of separateness from the whole is a kind of prison; healing reminds us of our place within the larger web of life. Research affirms this wisdom: feeling connected to others and the natural world enhances well-being, compassion, and resilience (Garland et al., 2015).

As we begin to embody the truth that we are inherently whole and worthy, the ego's veil lifts. We see ourselves and others with clearer, kinder eyes. Psychedelics can support this shift, deepening unconditional positive regard and helping integrate the parts of us that once felt fragmented. These moments of illumination expand perspective and strengthen trust in a larger unfolding.

Finally, the path of healing is rarely linear. Integration moves in waves—moments of progress, pauses, and unexpected turns. With support, those waves become the rhythm of transformation itself.

Managing Expectations

Returning to balance can be challenging. Past wounds and biological patterns may make inner exploration uncomfortable. Psychedelics can support healing, but they are not the answer alone—the real medicine lies in connection, both within and between us.

A common pitfall is turning the experience into more *doing*—judging, striving, or worrying that we didn't do it right. But again, healing isn't linear, and much of it unfolds beneath our awareness, as the nervous system learns new patterns of safety.

This is a time-released process. Insights may take days or weeks to emerge, and things often feel messier before they feel clearer. Years spent in survival mode don't unwind overnight. Change takes patience, safety, and relational support. That's why integration matters—and why community is essential.

Integration: Back to the Ordinary

Within your RTT Community of Practice, you'll be supported in weaving the psychedelic experience into daily life. Through compassionate witnessing and shared practice, you'll find the courage to live from a new perspective— reshaping how you relate to the past and present alike.

Change doesn't happen in isolation. It unfolds in the liminal space—the in-between—where old patterns dissolve and new ones take form. Though this space can feel uncertain, it's rich with possibility. To navigate it, we need anchors: relationships rooted in unconditional positive regard, and steady practices that help us reorient when uncertainty arises.

Throughout the program, you'll explore practices designed to regulate the nervous system and support integration. The key is to listen to your body— take what resonates and leave what doesn't. There's no one-size-fits-all approach. The goal is to build a personal toolkit that supports your unique way of *being*.

Let yourself soften into whatever unfolds. This surrender is the art of trust—a yielding that allows compassion to shape who we're becoming. Ease and discomfort both offer their own teachings, showing us where to lean in and where to let go.

When you feel stuck, as we all do at times, return to a question often shared by Julia, a senior RTT facilitator:

> *In any moment, am I more caught or more free?*
> *Am I playing out old patterns or moving with the currents of change?*

Integration is the return to the ordinary, carrying something of the extraordinary within you. Psychedelic experiences may open the door to profound insight, but it's in the everyday moments that those insights take root. With support, practice, and compassion, you begin to embody deeper truths. This is the work of becoming—not striving but softening into what's already there.

Preparing for the Journey Ahead

As we prepare to cross the threshold into non-ordinary states of consciousness, we enter a liminal space—a sacred in-between where transformation unfolds. This space isn't always comfortable, but it's often where the deepest healing begins. The following practices and protocols are offered not just as logistical steps, but as rituals to support your transition.

Appendix C: Intention Setting & Pillars of Strength

Intention setting and identifying pillars of strength are foundational RTT practices. Together, they support agency, alignment, and readiness—helping participants engage with medicine-assisted therapy from a place of safety, clarity, and self-compassion.

Intentions are the quiet forces that shape our experience—whether consciously or unconsciously. They guide our actions, influence our choices, and steer the course of healing. Even when we're not fully aware of them, intentions ripple forward, shaping how we engage with life.

Setting Intentions: Process over outcomes

Intentions work best when they focus on the process, not the outcome. It's natural to hope for certain results, but what we can actually influence are the inner qualities and ways of being that shape those results.

If you notice your intention leans toward an outcome, consider asking: *What quality do I need to cultivate to move toward this vision?*

For example, instead of saying, *I want to stop feeling anxious*, you might reframe it as, *I want to nurture calm and self-compassion.*

Intentions in psychedelic therapy vary widely. Some participants welcome open-ended exploration—inviting the medicine or their inner healing intelligence to guide the process. Others focus on cultivating specific qualities such as courage, forgiveness, or joy.

Begin by reflecting on your original intentions for joining this program:

- What brought you to this RTT journey?
- Who do you want to be at the end of the program? Be specific.
- What qualities need to expand for that future self to emerge?

When crafting your intention, consider:

- Is it personal—rooted in your own inner wisdom?
- Is it simple and specific—perhaps just a word or short phrase?
- Does it focus on what you want to move toward rather than what you want to avoid?

If several intentions come to mind, pause to listen to your body. Simply bring awareness to your breath and notice which intention feels most resonant or alive. Write it down. You can revisit and refine as you go.

You may find inspiration in broad themes like:

- Expanding awareness of your strengths
- Gaining insight into the roots of a life challenge

- Exploring an inspiration or desire that's calling you
- Inviting awareness of past trauma for healing
- Deepening self-compassion
- Cultivating forgiveness or compassion for others
- Deepening intimacy and connection
- Loosening attachment to unhelpful behaviours
- Accessing a sense of gratitude

As you set your intention, you can also ask that insights come gently and in ways that feel manageable. If you'd like support refining your intention, reach out to your facilitators—they're here to help. Once intentions are set, we turn to the inner anchors that help us stay grounded.

Pillars of Strength

Entering non-ordinary states of consciousness can feel both exciting and vulnerable. To prepare, identify the resources—inner and outer—that help you feel safe and grounded.

Our Communities of Practice offer a shared foundation of trust and connection that extends into medicine sessions. Alongside this collective support, notice which personal strengths you can lean on when activation arises. These might include a grounding practice, a trusted relationship, a spiritual guide, or an inner quality that brings comfort and stability.

Here are a few examples of where you can draw strength:

- Words & symbols: meaningful phrases, mantras, prayers
- Relational anchors: connection to loved ones, ancestors, or animals
- Inner qualities: resilience, courage, patience
- Spiritual traditions: cultural or spiritual practices that hold you
- Somatic tools: breathwork, grounding, body awareness, touchstones

These questions can help you dig a bit deeper to understand your resources:

- What helps you feel most secure when fear or uncertainty arises?
- What reminders or rituals help you return to your centre?
- Is there an object, image, or phrase that symbolizes your strength?

By setting intentions and leaning on our pillars of strength, we create a strong foundation, rooted in self-awareness and trust. These anchors help us navigate vulnerability, staying connected to what matters most.

Remember, you have resources and support around you. Ask for what you need, set boundaries that help you feel safe and in control. Healing often means learning to move in community—as the saying goes, we may go faster alone, but we go farther *together*.

Appendix D: Ketamine-assisted Therapy
by Dr. Pamela Kryskow, lead physician

Ketamine-assisted therapy offers another option for people who are living with persistent mental health symptoms that haven't improved with other treatments. In the RTT program, ketamine's dissociative and perspective-shifting effects can create space from past traumas and emotional patterns, making it easier for participants to process feelings, gain new insights, and support nervous system regulation.

About Ketamine

Ketamine is a medication that was discovered in 1956 and patented in 1962. Its first use was as an anesthetic for operations in 1970. The antidepressant effects of ketamine were noted around this time as well, and in the late 1980s, we learned of its usefulness for treating both alcohol and opiate use disorder.

Ketamine's psychedelic-like properties were also noted early on, but due to the growing stigma around psychedelic medicines at the time, it was labelled a *dissociative anesthetic* instead. Dissociative in this context refers to the way ketamine causes a sense of separation from one's regular thought patterns and bodily sensations. One may even have the sense of being temporarily separate from the body. It's not the same as when people are said to dissociate during, or following, a traumatic event.

In the RTT-KAT program, ketamine-assisted therapy (KAT) is an adjunct or companion to the therapeutic Community of Practice to help create conditions for insight, emotional processing, and nervous system regulation.

Other Treatment Options

Ketamine isn't the only treatment option for the challenges you're facing. Counselling, psychotherapy, other medications and supplements, ECT, Transcranial magnetic stimulation, and lifestyle changes such as meditation, mindfulness, exercise, yoga, tai chi, and Qi Gong can all assist in your journey.

On and Off-Label Uses

Ketamine is used 'off-label' in this program. *On-label* use of a medication refers to the use of the drug exactly as Health Canada has approved it—including prescribing it for the specific medical conditions (indications), for an approved dose, frequency, and patient group (age, sex, etc.). *Off-label* use is another **allowed use** of a medication when it's helpful for other conditions, at other doses, dosing frequencies, or other routes of administration (IV, by mouth, topical, injection, etc.) that were NOT tested in the clinical trials. It's commonly done by prescribers who judge it to be in a person's best interest, based on emerging evidence or clinical experience.

Ketamine currently has two 'on-label' uses:

- As an anesthetic, administered by injection or intravenous (IV).
- For treatment-resistant depression, administered intranasally (nasal spray).

There is strong evidence to support ketamine as an 'off-label' treatment for depression, chronic pain, anxiety, and acute suicidality. There is also growing evidence supporting the use of ketamine to treat eating disorders, end-of-life distress, substance use disorder, and Post Traumatic Stress Disorder (PTSD). And for symptoms like grief, burnout, or moral injury. Pain physicians are also using ketamine more and more frequently, instead of opioids, for acute pain treatment, such as after a knee operation.

In the RTT program, we use ketamine 'off-label' for numerous mental health conditions because there is strong evidence to support its usefulness.

The Science Behind How Ketamine Works (feel free to skip ahead if this isn't of interest to you)

There are four main theories as to how ketamine works as a psychedelic-like substance and may help in your healing journey. They are covered briefly below.

1. Ketamine blocks NMDA Receptors. It causes GABAergic inhibition, which gives a surge of glutamate release, and mood improves quickly because signalling is restored. This is likely why it's so helpful for depression.
2. Ketamine turns off your anti-reward centre, gives you a break from stress, facilitates emotional processing, and reduces avoidance states. This is called the lateral habenula theory. The understanding here is that anxiety and depression are manifestations of an overuse injury, just like a cashier who gets carpal tunnel syndrome from constantly scanning food items. The brain can be overused with anxiety or ruminating thoughts and be vulnerable to inflammation, just like the rest of the body.
3. Ketamine disrupts the connection between the cortex and the limbic system, giving you a time out from the ordinary mind, decreasing repetitive thoughts, and increasing cognitive flexibility. It gives you an opportunity to think of your past experiences differently.
4. Finally, ketamine stimulates BDNF, leading to new neural connections or neurogenesis, allowing you to make and strengthen new connections in the brain and learn new patterns of thinking and being. This can also help you learn a new skill faster.

Potential Benefits of Ketamine Over Time

Considering research and clinical outcomes, ketamine has the potential to:

- Facilitate the processing of emotions and memories
- Reduce the fear of painful emotions and memories
- Reprocess memories
- Release unprocessed emotions
- Help activate your inner healing intelligence
- Improve mood
- Increase insight
- Decrease anxiety
- Reduce emotional pain
- Reduce physical pain

You may notice changes immediately and/or over days, weeks, and months.

Potential Side Effects

Common temporary side effects of ketamine include:

- Temporary elevation in blood pressure and heart rate
- Poor balance — Movement in sessions is possible with assistance.
- Dizziness
- Blurred vision
- Double vision
- Tunnel vision
- Slurred speech
- Nausea*
- Anticipatory anxiety
- Agitation
- Confusion
- Pain at the injection site

*If you're someone who gets nauseated easily or experiences motion sickness, please let the RTT doctor know this during your appointment, so you can discuss the possible use of medications or supplements for nausea.

Uncommon Temporary Effects Include:

- Vomiting
- Insomnia the night following ketamine session
- Headache*
- Irritable bladder
- Loss of appetite
- Muscle tremors

*Migraines/headaches: Many people experience migraines as a health challenge. For some people participating in KAT, migraines get better. For others, they stay the same. There is no way to know which way it goes.

To lessen migraines, we suggest adding immediately to your daily supplements the following:

- Magnesium bisglycinate 200–400mg
- Vitamin B2 200-400mg
- Flushing Niacin 25mg slowly increasing to 500mg over weeks

If on the day of your ketamine session you feel a migraine starting, please take all your normal medications including triptans, acetaminophen, ibuprofen or other medications that can usually help you. These will not interact negatively with ketamine.

Very Rare Side Effects Include:

- Allergy to ketamine (treated with a drug called epinephrine)
- Laryngospasm — throat spasm; usually self-resolves or with support.

Our medical team is trained and prepared with appropriate medications and medical equipment for any emergencies that may arise.

Is Ketamine Addictive?

In our work, ketamine is used as an adjunct to therapy, not as a standalone substance. When the focus is on healing the root causes, misuse is rarely a concern. Ketamine in this context is not addictive; in fact, it can help resolve the traumas that often underlie substance misuse. When substances are approached with intention and transparency, they can become powerful tools for reducing harm and supporting recovery.

Health conditions that make taking ketamine unsafe:

If you have any of the following health conditions you must be medically cleared by your primary care doctor and our RTT doctor to be in our program. Unstable conditions must be stabilized and determined safe before proceeding.

- Unstable heart disease
- Untreated or poorly controlled hypertension
- Hyperthyroidism
- Psychosis
- Raised intraocular pressure (case by case consideration)
- Mania
- Pregnancy
- Liver disease (case by case consideration)
- Renal disease (case by case consideration)
- Intoxication on the day of the medicine session

You will be specifically screened for all these conditions in your doctor's referral, and through our intake process. Please let us know immediately if you have, or develop during our program, one of these conditions, so that we may make a safe or alternative treatment plan.

Medications

Medications of concern include benzodiazepines (lorazepam, clonazepam, diazepam, etc.), gabapentin, high dose naltrexone, Ozempic (and other GLP1 receptor agonists), stimulants, tramadol, opioids and some psychiatric medications. We will review your medications and supplements with you.

If you use any of these substances, they should have been listed on your referral form and reviewed during the intake process. If this was missed, please tell an RTT doctor immediately to make a safe treatment plan.

Consent for Treatment

Before your first ketamine session, you will receive instructions and information regarding the consent form that you will be required to sign to receive the ketamine therapy. You may withdraw your consent at any time before the injection of the medicine.

Preparing for Your Ketamine Session

Create space before your session for rest, relaxation, and reflection. In the days leading up, prioritize good sleep so you feel nourished and ready.

It's helpful to prepare for physical and emotional challenges that may show up during the KAT session. Consider practicing the tools offered in the program:

- 4/7/8 breath
- The daily energy routine
- EFT/tapping
- Butterfly Hug
- R.A.I.N.

Pre-session excitement or anxiety is normal and expected - this is an opportunity to try the strategies above.

You can't drive until after one full sleep. Please ensure you have a ride after, or we can help you arrange a taxi.

On the Day of Your Session:

Have a small amount of food 4-6 hours prior
You can have clear liquids up to 2 hours prior (light sips to relieve thirst)
- Avoid grapefruit juice & caffeine (if you will get a withdrawal headache, have ¼ of a cup of your caffeinated beverage)
- Avoid stimulants (if possible)
- Wear comfortable clothing & bring layers

137

What to Bring to Your Ketamine Session

We provide mats, weighted blankets, eye coverings, and headphones for your use during the session.

Please bring your own pillow, socks or slippers, water, a sweater/layers, and healthy snacks.

Consider also bringing additional blankets, items of support or significance such as photos, and a journal and pen. If you anticipate feeling uncomfortable lying down, please bring any extra pillows/bolsters that may help, or anything else that will make you feel more comfortable. Ketamine can give you the sensation of feeling cold, so you may want a few extra layers.

Ketamine Session Information

Your three ketamine sessions will be with your small group. You will all experience the medicine together at the same time. The session will be led by your small group facilitators and will be supported by various members of our team. You will have met everyone in the room on-screen during our Community of Practice meetings.

On the day of the ketamine session, you will arrive at the wellness centre for a check-in. This involves having your blood pressure and heart rate checked. Your blood pressure needs to be in the normal range to have ketamine therapy. If you arrive and it's outside our treatment range, we will help you utilize various relaxation techniques to help you lower your blood pressure. If it's still high, we have the option of offering you either clonidine or captopril - two medications that are used to lower blood pressure and will not interfere with ketamine. If we can't get your blood pressure in range, we will have to postpone your ketamine session.

You will see an RTT doctor for any final questions and to confirm your ketamine dose.

You then will settle into the ceremony room with your group. It will be a large room, with mats on the floor for each participant, and floor cushions for your facilitators and other team members.

Medication Dose and Administration

The amount of ketamine you receive is partly based on your weight, your experience with non-ordinary states and partly based on your intention for your medicine session. You will discuss your dose prior to your session with an RTT doctor during an online appointment. There, you will have an opportunity to ask any remaining questions and together decide on a dose based on your priorities, intentions, previous experience, and comfort level. On the day of your session at the health centre, you will have another opportunity to meet with your RTT doctor for any new questions and confirm the dose.

138

Please know that the dose you decide on is the right dose. No matter what, the medicine will meet you exactly where you are and support you on your journey.

You will receive the ketamine in an intramuscular injection into your gluteal muscle (buttock). When it's time to administer the medication, we will ask you to lie on your side, so a doctor or nurse can give the injection into your buttock. This will be done discreetly. You also have the option of a deltoid/shoulder injection - please discuss this with your RTT doctor in your appointment if you're interested in this option.

The injection will take about 20 seconds. You will then lay down and get comfortable with your eye shades, headphones and blanket on. Music will be playing in your headphones and in the room. A unique playlist is curated for each ketamine session. Within 2-4 minutes you will begin to feel the effects of the ketamine. Usually, the first sensation you feel is relaxation. You will feel the medicine most strongly 40-90 minutes after your injection.

You may experience an out-of-body sensation, formlessness, visual hallucinations, a sense of timelessness, a disruption or dissolution of negative feelings, relaxation from ordinary concerns, or a break from the constant stream of thoughts in your head. You may also have visions, relive memories, or you may experience no visuals and darkness. All experiences are normal.

You may hear crying, laughter, or conversation from others in the room. At times, there may be movement or sounds as the team supports people with their physical and emotional needs. Please know the team will tend to everyone's needs, so you can simply stay focused on your own journey.

You may be accustomed to caring for others in your day-to-day life. It can be a powerful experience to release your role as a caregiver, and to just BE in a journey. It's okay to trust that others can navigate their own experience, and that the team can support whatever arises. Allow yourself to let go of any responsibility for others in the room. You don't have to DO anything; you can BE in your experience. This is your time.

The overall ketamine session is 4-5 hours; however, you will still feel the effects of the ketamine for several hours after you leave. This is why you must not drive, operate equipment, or do anything that could be compromised by your being tired and/or uncoordinated following your session. Because you will be unsafe to drive yourself home, you must have someone pick you up from the health centre. We can assist you in calling a taxi if needed.

Your Ketamine Experience

Everybody's experience is different. Whatever your experience is, it's what you need to take you to the next stages of YOUR healing journey.

The ketamine sessions are an opportunity to trust and invest in your own deep processes of growth and healing. You may be worried that the ketamine 'won't work'. This is a common concern. It may not look like what you expect, but trust that you will get the learnings or experience that you need. Trust that your inner healing intelligence knows what you need to heal.

Think of hiking to a lake 5km away—you don't take one step and end up at the lake. Instead, the path winds, there are hills and valleys, and all along the way there are interesting things to see. Each step along the path is part of the journey. Ketamine will help your mind, body and spirit prioritize what needs to be attended to first, what steps are next along the path.

Some of you may have a very 'big' experience—your path might be filled with visuals, memories, profound insights. For others it may feel subtle—a quiet stroll. Some may feel nothing happened at all except a rest.

If you're in a challenging moment, start by reminding yourself that you're physically safe. Explore what the experience might be teaching you, what questions it raises, and what steps could help you move through it. If you need support to trust and let go, ask for help from the team or return to your pillars of strength. Curiosity for all that comes up is a helpful tool.

As you emerge from your experience, please remember *all* experiences are valuable and exactly what each person needs. Try to avoid comparing your experience to others. Each person is unique and so will be their experience.

We spend time setting intentions for the medicine session. It can be helpful, but it's important to let go of the *outcome* of your ketamine session. Practice letting go of expectations, trusting that whatever arises is exactly right for you. In this place of surrender, you can *receive* what's offered to you.

Integration

The 36 to 48 hours following a medicine session experience is an important opportunity to engage in self-care, practice new patterns, engage in creative or artistic activities and begin to establish new neural pathways. You may hear us speaking of this time period as one of heightened **opportunity for change**. Neuroplasticity is the brain's ability to modify, change, and adapt both structure and function.

Create a cozy spot where you can settle in and rest without rushing. We strongly encourage you to protect the following day with rest and gentleness. Previous participants have stated that having two days after their session off work was helpful.

140

It may be important for you to flex your schedule and expectations of yourself to accommodate and care for yourself as new awareness and needs arise.

The following are some suggestions for the days following your session:

- Create a calm & relaxing spot in your home
- Limit outside distractions as much as possible
- Consider taking a break from social media for a few days (or weeks)
- Eat nourishing, healthy foods (vegetables, protein, fruits, healthy fats)
- Drink a lot of water or other refreshing fluids
- Journal
- Engage creatively—paint, draw, sculpt, make music, dance
- Do light exercise - walking, stretching
- Spend time in nature – forests, by water, gardens
- Daydream
- Meditate - if this is new to you, there are numerous guided meditations online.
- Supplement with magnesium-it can be helpful for relaxation and sleep

To assist in integrating insights from the medicine sessions, we offer online integration sessions in the two days following your session. Days and times of integration sessions will be sent to you in an email from our team. While these sessions are optional, we strongly encourage you to attend one or all of them, even if just to listen. Integration sessions are an opportunity to talk about your experience, be witnessed by others, and be a witness for the experience of others.

Appendix E: Psilocybin-assisted Therapy

by Dr. Pamela Kryskow, lead physician

Psilocybin-assisted therapy aligns naturally with RTT's focus on awareness, compassion, non-attachment, and alignment. Psilocybin's introspective and insight-oriented effects can open access to deeper layers of healing, especially when the experience is supported and integrated through relational and somatic practices.

About Psilocybin

Psilocybin is known as one of the 'classic' psychedelics and is derived from mushrooms of the genus Psilocybe (and others) and has a long history across the globe for cultural healing and spiritual practices. While it has been used for spiritual and medicinal purposes for many years in many cultures, here in Canada, it hasn't yet been approved for therapeutic purposes by Health Canada. There are over 140 clinical trials on the therapeutic benefits of psilocybin in process as of this writing.

How Psilocybin Works

Psilocybin is a partial serotonin agonist that binds to receptors in the brain responsible for mood and anxiety regulation, including those in the prefrontal cortex. While the molecular mechanisms remain unclear, effects produce what's commonly described as a mystical-like, non-ordinary experience, which in turn facilitates antidepressant and anti-anxiety benefits. Psilocybin can also bring about different states of consciousness, including what might be described as spiritual or mystical awareness. These experiences can support new insights, greater access to and/or a reorientation of memories and thought patterns, and a different sense of self and reality. In a safe environment, with therapeutic support, working with psilocybin can help individuals heal and transform, finding greater peace and compassion. Such journeys tend to lead to a positive change in outlook and character, and relieve symptoms of depression, PTSD, anxiety, and other difficult states of mind and heart. Additionally, research confirms that it helps resolve the trauma at the root cause of most substance use disorders.

Psilocybin's period of duration varies, but it's usually four to eight hours. The experience is a time-out from our ordinary state of mind. Characteristically, it provides relaxation from ordinary concerns while maintaining conscious awareness of the flow of mind. This relief tends to lead to a disruption of negative feelings and obsessional preoccupations. It's uniquely impactful when coupled with exploration and experience of other possible states of consciousness. Members of the treatment team act as facilitators of the experience, preparing you and supporting your process.

Symptoms and Conditions Psilocybin May be Useful For

There is growing evidence for the use of psilocybin for both mental health and physical health challenges. At the time of the printing of this book, there are over 140 clinical trials in process registered at ClinicalTrials.gov.

In RTT, treatment through the Special Access Program is available for symptoms such as treatment-resistant depression, end-of-life existential distress, and cluster headaches.

There's also evidence of benefit for other conditions, including:

- Depression, Major Depressive Disorder, and Dysthymia
- Anxiety, social, and general
- Disordered Eating
- Grief
- PTSD
- Substance Use Disorders, including alcohol, tobacco, opioids
- Obsessive Compulsive Disorder
- Cognitive Impairment related to Traumatic Brain Injury
- Dementia and memory issues

Who Should Not Use Psilocybin

- Personal or family history of psychotic disorders such as schizophrenia or schizoaffective disorder.
- Bipolar disorder or a history of mania/hypomania
- Pregnancy or breastfeeding – Limited data on fetal or infant exposure.
- Severe cardiovascular conditions because psilocybin can transiently increase heart rate and blood pressure.
- MAO inhibitors – Risk of life-threatening serotonin syndrome.
- Epilepsy/seizure disorders – May lower seizure threshold.
- Allergy or hypersensitivity to psilocybin or mushroom components.
- Severe liver or kidney disease
- Severe psychiatric instability (e.g., active suicidal ideation).

Medications that May Interact or Interfere with Psilocybin Therapy

- Lithium – increases risk of seizure
- Tramadol – increases risk of seizure
- SSRIs – may diminish effects in some people
- Buspirone – may diminish effects
- Typical Antipsychotics – may increase anxiety
- Triptans – additive vasoconstriction
- Diclofenac, probenecid, cinacalcet – may diminish effects.

Potential Benefits of Psilocybin Over Time

Psilocybin's antidepressant properties may help improve mood by reducing symptoms of depression and anxiety. Many individuals also report gaining fresh perspectives on themselves, their emotions, and life challenges. Beyond mood enhancement, psilocybin often promotes a deeper sense of well-being, greater cognitive flexibility, and increased openness to new experiences.

Potential Effects of Psilocybin

After ingesting psilocybin medicine, it's common at 10 – 40 minutes to feel the sensation of butterflies or of nausea in your stomach. This is a signal that psilocybin is binding your receptors, and your experience is beginning.

During the session the following may be experienced:

- Visual imagery: Seeing colorful, geometric patterns or vivid mental scenes.
- Synesthesia: Experiencing blending of senses, such as "hearing colours" or "tasting sounds."
- Connectedness: Feelings of deep peace, joy, and unity with others or the world.
- Ego dissolution: A loss or loosening of the usual sense of self or personal boundaries.
- Mystical-type experiences: Profound states often described as spiritual or transcendent, which can change worldview.
- Intense feelings: You may feel anxiety, fear, or distress, especially with loss of control or difficult emotions.
- Physical discomfort: A result of processing emotions or memories

It's normal after the session or the next day to have a headache. It's fine to take ibuprofen or acetaminophen (if safe for you) to resolve the headache.

How a Psilocybin-assisted Therapy (PaT) Session Works

During your PaT treatment sessions, you will be accompanied by a medical clinician and a PaT trained therapeutic sitter. Once you take the psilocybin, most effects will last between four to eight hours. Unlike other forms of therapy, PaT is largely an inner journey. To support an inward focus and minimize external distraction, instrumental music will be played, and we encourage the use of eye shades. It's not necessary to talk through your experience while the medicine effects are unfolding.

There will be an opportunity to share and process your experience as the effects of the medicine wane and later wear off. That said, the clinician and therapist are available to support you at any time if needed.

Transformation can come while preparing for your psychedelic experience (see **Appendix C** for intention setting), during your experience, and following your experience during integration. We provide here some thoughts and ideas about each of these phases. Hold them gently and run them through your own discernment process. Keep what works and set down what doesn't.

Preparation

Minimize physical distractions as much as possible by ensuring you address your body's needs and comfort preferences leading up to your session. This care includes wearing layers to keep you at a comfortable temperature and using pillows or bolsters as needed.

Eat and drink clear fluids very lightly before the session so your body can absorb the psilocybin more easily.

Take your regular medication unless you have been advised by the RTT doctors to withhold something specific. If you have specific medications you feel you will need, please bring them.

Get a good night's sleep before the session.

Before your session, it's helpful to prepare for physical and emotional challenges that may arise during the PaT session. The body may experience stress: this is an excellent opportunity to practice self-regulation strategies. The body may feel strong emotional sensations: this happening is a fantastic thing and an opportunity to allow an old wound to heal. Because psilocybin facilitates a sense of non-attachment toward emotions (a concept discussed in more detail in the main text), you have an opportunity to feel or witness intense emotions without experiencing them as a threat.

During the session, you will most likely be lying down on a comfortable mat. If you prefer a cot or semi-reclining chair, please let the team know. We want you to be as comfortable as possible.

What To Bring

We provide mats, weighted blankets, eye shades, and headphones. Please bring a water bottle, pillow, socks/slippers, and a healthy snack for after the session (like cut-up fruit, nuts, crackers, etc.). Consider also bringing your journal and pen, photographs, art supplies if you like to draw, and other touchstones you may want with you. If you have a favourite pair of eyeshades, bring those too.

Your Psilocybin Experience

During the psilocybin session, we first get settled into the ceremony room, do a grounding exercise, discuss your intentions, your pillars of strengths and any supports from your therapists that you would like for when you take the medicine (examples of support are covered in **Appendix G**).

Surrender as much as you can into whatever experience you're given. We encourage you to go 'down and in' listening to yourself rather than 'up and out' in conversation. Avoid the urge to talk or connect with others about your experience while you're still in it. The deeper and more silent your experience, the more meaningful and transformative it can be.

A trusted mantra is *Trust, Let Go, Be Curious*. You can ask, *what do I need to learn from this experience?* You might even ask what comes up or any challenges a question, which can promote non-attachment and compassion for what's arising. If you need support to trust and let go, the team is there to support you. Please ask for help from the team or try returning to your curiosity and/or pillars of strength.

Although we spent time setting intentions for the journey, *at this point it's important to let go of the outcome and know that your mind, body, and spirit know exactly what your priorities are.*

After Your Psilocybin Session

You can't drive until the next day. Please ensure you have a ride after, or we can help you arrange a taxi.

Integration

Around 6 hours after you have taken the psilocybin, it will wear off and you will gradually come back into ordinary time and place. You will bring with you everything you have experienced and learned.

While we are still together and before we end the session, we will have a transition circle for sharing. If you are not ready or find it difficult to speak about your experience during this closing portion, please honour that. You might not yet have the clarity or words to describe your experience. Alternatively, you might be excited and ready to share. Give yourself time and space to navigate this period. Trust yourself to know what you need during this time.

The 36 to 48 hours following a medicine session experience is an important opportunity to engage in self-care, practice new patterns, and begin to establish new neural pathways. You may hear us speaking of this period as one of heightened **neuroplasticity**. Neuroplasticity is simply the brain's ability to modify, change, and adapt both structure and function.

Create a cozy spot where you can land gently and give yourself time to breathe. If possible, keep the next day clear—make space for rest and let your body and mind settle without rushing back into the noise of daily life. Previous participants have stated that having two days after their session off work was helpful. It may become important for you to flex your schedule and expectations of yourself to accommodate and care for yourself as new awareness and needs arise.

146

The following are some suggestions for the days following your session:

- Create a calm & relaxing spot in your home
- Limit outside distractions as much as possible
- Consider taking a break from social media for a few days (or weeks)
- Eat nourishing, healthy foods (vegetables, protein, fruits, healthy fats)
- Drink a lot of water or other refreshing fluids
- Journal
- Engage creatively—paint, draw, sculpt, make music, dance
- Do light exercise - walking, stretching
- Spend time in nature – forests, by water, gardens
- Daydream
- Meditate - if this is new to you, there are numerous guided meditations online.
- Supplement with magnesium-it can be helpful for relaxation and sleep.

Integration happens as we embody our new insights, which then leads to new behaviours. It happens when we settle into and practice new ways of being in the world. Trust your intuition, listen to your body, and engage in activities that feel inspiring rather than obligatory.

When your insights start to resonate strongly and feel integrated within you, try writing them down. Writing can connect your new understanding and bodily awareness to how you express and live those insights in your daily life. To integrate these awarenesses further, you can share them with a trusted friend, family member, or therapist.

Appendix F: MDMA-assisted Therapy

MDMA-assisted therapy can help people feel more open, connected, and less afraid—making it a natural fit with healing spaces that focus on relationships and resilience. The work happens within a structured, supportive setting, and always moves at the pace of the participant, honoring readiness and choice.

About MDMA

MDMA (3,4-methylenedioxymethamphetamine) is known to support emotional openness, empathy, and clarity. First synthesized in 1912, it was used for therapeutic purposes in the 1970s before being restricted. Today, MDMA is again being studied for its potential role in supporting healing, particularly for those processing emotional, physical, or sexual trauma.

Trauma can leave the body and mind in a prolonged state of fear, even after danger has passed. This heightened state can make traditional talk therapy feel overwhelming or unsafe. MDMA-assisted therapy offers an alternative approach. In a professionally guided setting, the medicine may help calm the nervous system and reduce fear, creating conditions where exploring painful memories and emotions feels more manageable.

Rather than erasing the past, MDMA can help us approach it with more clarity and compassion. When the emotions tied to old experiences are finally acknowledged and processed, something shifts—there's more room to breathe, to understand, and to see new possibilities. The pain doesn't vanish, but its intensity softens. Instead of defining us, it becomes a part of our story we can draw wisdom and resilience from.

Clinical trials have shown promising results: after three sessions, 67% of participants no longer met PTSD criteria, and 87% experienced significant symptom reduction. While MDMA is not yet widely approved for therapeutic use in Canada, it has been designated by the U.S. FDA as a Breakthrough Therapy based on its effectiveness in clinical trials. When used with care, intention, and professional support, MDMA-assisted therapy may help access parts of us that are often difficult to reach through conversation alone.

How MDMA Works

MDMA works in unique ways that help you feel safe, open, and connected. Unlike classic psychedelics like psilocybin, MDMA typically doesn't produce visions or major shifts in perception. Instead, many describe the experience as one of emotional clarity, self-acceptance, and grounded openness.

In a safe therapeutic environment, MDMA can soften the protective walls built through fear or trauma. Through the process you may feel more connected—to yourself, to loved ones, and to the world around you.

Support in the Healing Process:

- Emotional balance: MDMA increases serotonin, dopamine, and norepinephrine—neurochemicals that help regulate mood, energy, and emotional resilience. This can create a sense of well-being that supports deeper therapeutic work.
- Connection and trust (improving congruence): The medicine boosts bonding hormones like oxytocin and prolactin, helping you feel connected to people, including your facilitators, your loved ones, and yourself.
- Reduced fear responses: MDMA calms the amygdala, the part of the brain that signals danger. With this alarm system quieted, you can revisit painful memories without becoming overwhelmed.
- Sense of coherence: By strengthening communication between the thinking and emotional areas of the brain, MDMA helps you stay present and reflective while engaging with emotions. This balance supports healing and the creation of new, empowering narratives.

In short, MDMA doesn't do the healing for you—it helps you meet your pain with clarity, compassion, and courage. When you are held within a safe and intentional therapeutic container, supported by strong facilitators, this experience can be a powerful catalyst for transformation.

Potential Side Effects and Support

Most people find MDMA sessions safe and supportive, though your body may respond in ways that feel a little unfamiliar or uncomfortable. These effects are usually mild and temporary.

To help ease any discomfort, supplements may be offered during your session. These are selected thoughtfully to support your body and nervous system.

You might notice:

- A faster heartbeat
- Jaw tension or tight muscles
- Feeling warmer or cooler than usual
- Mild nausea
- Sensitivity to light or sound
- Feeling tired or emotionally low in the days after

If anything feels uncomfortable, let your facilitators know right away—they're there to support you, and asking for help is a great way to build those self-compassion muscles.

What Does an MDMA-Assisted Therapy Session Look Like?

A typical MDMA-assisted therapy session often lasts 6–8 hours and is guided by trained facilitators—therapists and clinicians who provide a supportive, attentive presence. Their role is to help create a safe environment and offer guidance if challenges arise, such as emotional intensity or uncertainty.

Before introducing the medicine, your care team will check your blood pressure and heart rate. You'll then be invited to engage in grounding practices—such as mindful breathing, gentle movement, or reflecting on your intentions—to help establish a sense of safety and readiness.

Once MDMA is taken, its effects usually begin within 30 to 60 minutes. The experience tends to deepen gradually, often peaking between 1.5 and 2.5 hours after ingestion. During this time, some people report feeling more open, emotionally warm, and connected, which can support the therapeutic process and carry into later integration work.

Throughout the session, you may alternate between quiet, inward reflection and dialogue with your therapists. Some moments may feel introspective, while others invite exploration of memories, emotions, or insights that arise. Music is often part of the setting, chosen to support focus and evoke feelings that can guide the process.

Your facilitators will remain present the entire time—offering prompts, reassurance, or simply sitting with you in silence when that's what's needed. Their role isn't to direct your experience, but to support you in following your own inner healing intelligence. They will invite you to soften into whatever arises with curiosity and trust. Strong emotions may surface, but the MDMA medicine often creates enough space for you to face them without being overwhelmed. This is an opportunity for you to let old wounds be met with a new compassion rather than fear.

Let go as much as you can of expectation or outcome. Trust that what emerges in your journey is meaningful for your growth. If you find yourself grasping or resisting, practice curiosity—ask what the feeling might be showing you. Remember that you're not alone. Your facilitators are with you, and you can always ask for support.

After the peak, you'll have time to integrate what has emerged—whether that's through conversation, journaling, or simply resting. In the days and weeks that follow, integration sessions help you process what came up and begin applying your insights into daily life.

MDMA doesn't do the healing for us—it simply creates the conditions that make healing more accessible. With the right support, many people find they can face experiences that once felt overwhelming, allowing emotions to move through with more clarity, courage, and self-compassion.

Consent and Therapeutic Touch

At every stage, you have full control over what happens in the space—including whether or not you want therapeutic touch as part of your experience.

Before the session begins, your facilitators will talk with you about the possible role of touch in the therapeutic process. They will give clear demonstrations of what's available. Examples include a hand on the shoulder, holding a hand during emotional moments, or a grounding touch to help you feel safe. You'll be invited to share your preferences, boundaries, and any concerns you may have. Nothing is assumed, and nothing will happen without your clear, informed consent.

You can change your mind about touch at any time. If you've given consent and later decide you'd rather not be touched, your choice will be respected immediately and without question. If, in a moment, you feel that touch might be supportive, you're welcome to ask for it.

However, any boundaries you set before taking the medicine will remain in place for the entire session, even if you change your mind while in the non-ordinary state. This ensures that all parts of you—including the ones that may be quieter or less able to speak clearly during the experience—are fully respected and protected.

The goal is to ensure that any physical contact is always in service of your healing and always aligned with your comfort. Your facilitators are trained to listen deeply—not just to your words, but to your body language and energy—and to respond with care, presence, and respect.

This is your journey. You set the pace, and you define the boundaries. We're here to support you in a way that feels safe, empowering, and attuned to your needs.

Preparing your Body

To help your body receive the medicine comfortably, eat lightly before your session. Consider soup or a light snack. Continue taking your regular medications unless your doctor advises otherwise. Aim for a good night's sleep the evening before. If possible, leave the next day unscheduled for resting and integration.

You may also be encouraged to take specific supplements—such as magnesium or vitamins—to support your nervous system and help ease any physical discomfort during the session.

Preparing your mind is also important. Spend a little time reflecting on your intention for this work (**see Appendix C**). Reflect on what you're ready to invite in—healing, compassion, clarity, or courage.

Transportation and Safety After Your Session

Please arrange a ride to and from your MDMA-assisted therapy session. The effects of the medicine can linger beyond the session itself. **You are not permitted to drive until you've had a full night's sleep**.

What To Bring

We provide comfortable mats, blankets, weighted blankets, eye shades, and headphones. You may want to bring:

- A water bottle and snack for after the session (fruit, nuts, crackers).
- A pillow, socks/slippers, or a blanket to help you feel cozy.
- Wear/bring light layers that can be adjusted if you're warm or cool.
- A journal and pen for capturing insights after the session.
- Personal touchstones, such as photographs or meaningful objects, if these feel supportive.

Integration

In the 24 to 48 hours after your MDMA session, you may feel tender, open, and deeply connected. This is a precious window of heightened emotional receptivity. We encourage you to move gently, protect your time with rest, and lean into practices that help you carry your insights into daily life.

Here are some supportive ways to integrate:

- Listening to the session playlist again – music helps reconnect you to the experience.
- Reflection – journalling, meditation, or simply resting in silence.
- Creative expression – painting, music, dance, or writing can help you process and express what you've felt.
- Nourishment – eat wholesome food, drink water, and tend to your body with care.
- Connection – if comfortable, share your experience with trusted others or in integration sessions.
- Movement – walking, stretching, or breathwork to settle your nervous system.

Integration is about living our insights, not just thinking about them. It's letting new ways of being take root in daily life. Sharing our journey and allowing others to witness us creates support around us and helps sustain meaningful change.

Hold this work gently. Trust your pace. Keep what feels true and release what doesn't.

And remember your resources and the supports around you. Healing is often about learning *how* to travel *together*.

Appendix G: Touch & Energy Medicine During Your Medicine Session

by Helen Watler and Darlus Jonsson, somatic energy practitioners

In addition to the medicine itself, therapeutic touch and energy work offer vital layers of support during your session. Throughout the experience, energy practitioners and facilitators are present to help regulate the nervous system, deepen safety, and support emotional release.

While some participants lie still on the mat, headphones on and eyes covered for the duration of the session, others report benefit from therapeutic touch.

Touch during RTT sessions can include handholding, a reassuring hand on the shoulder, or a calming touch to the forehead. Holding the ankles or soles of the feet can support grounding, while placing hands on the chest—front or back—can help regulate the heart's energy field.

Energy workers may also use acupressure or neuro-lymphatic points on the head, hands, legs or feet to support emotional release. Beyond physical contact, energy work may be offered in the energetic field surrounding the body, providing comfort and connection without direct touch.

Touch is offered only when necessary and with your permission. We verify your consent with you before the medicine session. That said, if there are immediate concerns for your physical safety, we may need to touch you to keep you or others around you safe.

During the session, therapeutic touch can offer a corrective experience— reminding the body it's not alone, that others are with you, keeping you safe. This physical care can help rewrite old stories of separation and isolation.

Asking for physical support can expand your window of tolerance, affirming that you're worthy of support. To create this sense of security in the body, you may ask for physical touch during your session.

Alternatively, it may be empowering to set a boundary, requesting no touch at all. That may be what you need to instill a feeling of security in the body. Please know, we will honour your requests, and we are here to support throughout your session.

Videos will be available to all KAT/PAT participants explaining the therapeutic touch and energy medicine supports offered by facilitators during medicine sessions.

Appendix H: Music as Medicine
by Phillip Dames, Operations Lead & Playlist Curator

Music in RTT supports preparation, emotional regulation, presence, and integration. Curated playlists help metabolize strong emotions and sensations, deepen connection to the inner healing intelligence, and expand the window of tolerance.

We all hold stuck energy in the body. The medicine will show you where it is; the music will meet you there and help move it. It's a tool—when you meet the music with presence, your inner healing intelligence takes it from there.

What is music?

Music is medicine

Music is tangible

Music is a touch point in time

Music pulls you into active listening

Music is art

Music is connection

Music is vulnerability

Music is integration

Music is meant to be shared

Music is love

Music moves energy

With intention and a safe and secure environment, music helps move strong emotions and sensations. It fosters *heartfulness* and, alongside regulation practices, can expand our window of tolerance. This can be especially helpful for those who have been immersed in trauma-laden environments (Bensimon, 2020) or who live with the effects of post-traumatic stress (Beck et al., 2021; Macfarlane et al., 2019).

By making space for the feelings and sensations music can elicit, we learn to make space for emotion in our daily lives. It reminds us *how* to actively listen; to be *fully* present. In that presence, curiosity grows, distractions fade, and time feels fluid. Rather than anticipating what comes next, we learn to rest *in* the moment, allowing the music to guide us—meeting whatever arises.

In this way, music can be an integral part of healing. It creates a *touch point in time* we can return to through sound and memory. Layered, textured tracks deepen this effect, opening pathways for connection. Our bodies can recall these moments, even when the mind can't.

154

Music is one of the most powerful companions in medicine-assisted therapy. It shapes mood, evokes memory, and guides emotion and energy as it moves through the body. The combination of *set* (your mindset and intentions) and *setting* (your environment, tools, and supports) creates the foundation for this process—music is what brings it all to life.

Go Inside

Begin by turning inward. Close your eyes, tune into the music, which can help you tune out the external world. As you are pulled into presence, you can listen to your inner landscape.

Choose Wisely

Select music that moves you—sounds that awaken sensations while opening your heart space. Instrumental or wordless music often works best, allowing your inner voice to emerge clearly. If you choose songs with lyrics, make sure their message aligns with your values and intentions.

Resonance

Like musical instruments, we attune to each other and to sound. The resonance you feel with certain music can ripple outward, shaping the emotional tone of your environment. Choose tracks that your body naturally responds to, as resonance amplifies connection and presence.

Tension and Release

Music that moves through tension and release mirrors the emotional process of healing. Tracks rich with *timbre*—varied tones and textures—can help you move through emotional layers with more depth and fluidity.

Texture and Tone

Ambient music is often a good place to start. Its spacious, overtone-rich quality can create a sense of openness. Natural sounds like birdsong, rainfall, or flowing water can enhance that sense of space and calm.

Body Resonance

Different instruments engage different parts of the body. Deep bass tones can ground you in your centre, connect you to the land, and awaken the heart—what Elder Geraldine Manson calls the *pilot light* within. The sound of a cello or bowed string can open the heart, while higher tones—like a violin or flute—can lift the mind and expand awareness.

Finding tracks that have a structure of tension and release allows you to move through different emotional processes. Having a higher level of timbre helps in this process as well.

Ambient music often provides a nice blend of overtone-based music that's rich in timbre. The layers of various textures create spaciousness. Mixing in natural sounds like birds, rain, or running water can increase spaciousness.

Use different instruments and textures in the music to activate different parts of your body. Strong beats send vibrations into your centre, reminding you of your inner resources. The sound of a bow on a stringed bass can be resonant with your heart, or a violin may stimulate your mind.

Working with Strong Emotions/Sensations

If strong sensations come up, this is an excellent time to use your regulation practices (softening tension with breath, EFT/tapping, stretching, physical activity, the butterfly hug, dance, sigh, etc.). Also, notice what song is playing when the sensations arise, approaching this information with curiosity. You might think of each song as a scene in a movie. Ultimately, each scene ends, as will each song, and the emotions it evokes.

Use R.A.I.N. (described earlier), which reminds us to recognize, allow, investigate, and nurture what comes up for tending and releasing.

Get outside and move! Combining music with nature and movement can be a profound mixture. Physical movement allows for energetic release, which creates space. In that space, music can support a process of *unfolding*.

Notice the tracks that spark insight or awaken your felt senses. Return to the ones that move you—your mind may forget, but your body remembers. If strong emotions arise while listening, revisit the track later; this helps integrate what's emerging.

Begin with gentle music that offers comfort rather than stimulation, as activating sounds can feel overwhelming at first—like shaking a snow globe. As you practice and develop a relationship with music, you will be more able to allow strong sensations to come and go, trusting you have the inner and outer resources (security and regulating tools) to navigate whatever arises.

Don't be afraid to play the music loud. It helps your body to feel the music, to become one with it.

Music is a powerful tool for both preparation and integration. To explore curated Roots to Thrive playlists—designed to accompany different psychedelic medicines—scan the QR code to visit our Spotify page.

References

Acoba, E. F. (2024). Social support and mental health: The mediating role of perceived stress. *Frontiers in Psychology, 15*, 1330720. https://doi.org/10.3389/fpsyg.2024.1330720

Aktaş, G. K., & İlgin, V. E. (2023). The effect of deep breathing exercise and 4-7-8 breathing techniques applied to patients after bariatric surgery on anxiety and quality of life. *Obesity Surgery, 33*, 920–929. https://doi.org/10.1007/s11695-022-06364-3

Alameda, C., Sanabria, D., & Ciria, L. F. (2022). The brain in flow: A systematic review on the neural basis of the flow state [Preprint]. *Mind, Brain & Behaviour Research Centre, University of Granada.*

Anālayo, B. (2019). Meditation on the breath: Mindfulness and focused attention. *Mindfulness, 10*(11), 2430–2439. https://doi.org/10.1007/s12671-019-01169-9

Antonovsky, A. (1979). *Health, stress, and coping.* Jossey-Bass.

Antonovsky, A. (1987). *Unraveling the mystery of health: How people manage stress and stay well.* Jossey-Bass.

Artigas, L., Jarero, I., Mauer, M., López Cano, T., & Alcalá, N. (2000). EMDR and traumatic stress after natural disasters: Integrative treatment protocol and the butterfly hug. Poster presented at the EMDRIA Conference, Toronto, Ontario, Canada.

Balban, M. Y., Neri, E., Kogon, M. M., Weed, L., Nouriani, B., Jo, B., Holl, G., Zeitzer, J. M., Spiegel, D., & Huberman, A. D. (2023). Brief structured respiration practices enhance mood and reduce physiological arousal. *Cell Reports Medicine, 4*(1), 100895. https://doi.org/10.1016/j.xcrm.2022.100895

Barnett, J. E., & Homany, G. (2022). The new self-care: It's not all about you. *Practice Innovations, 7*(4), 313–326. https://doi.org/10.1037/pri0000190

Bartlett, M. Y., & DeSteno, D. (2006). Gratitude and prosocial behaviour. *Psychological Science, 17*(4), 319–325. https://doi.org/10.1111/j.1467-9280.2006.01705.x

Battaglini, C. A., Zareian, S., & LeMoult, J. (2025). Intra- versus interpersonal emotion regulation: Associations with affect reactivity and biological stress responses. *Psychophysiology.* https://doi.org/10.1111/psyp.14853

Beck, B. D., Meyer, S. L., Simonsen, E., Søgaard, U., Petersen, I., Arnfred, S. M. H., Tellier, T., & Moe, T. (2021). Music therapy was noninferior to verbal standard treatment of traumatized refugees in mental health care: Results from a randomized clinical trial. *European Journal of Psychotraumatology, 12*(1), Article 1863579. https://doi.org/10.1080/20008198.2020.1863579

Bekkali, S., Youssef, G. J., Donaldson, P. H., Albein-Urios, N., Hyde, C., Carter, O., & Lubman, D. I. (2021). Is the mirror neuron system involved in empathy? A systematic review and meta-analysis. *Neuropsychology Review, 31*(1), 14–57. https://doi.org/10.1007/s11065-020-09452-6

Bell, C. (1992). *Ritual theory, ritual practice.* Oxford University Press.

Benedetto, L., Ingrassia, M., & Tosto, C. (2024). Self-compassion and perfectionism: The mediating role of psychological flexibility. *Current Psychology, 43*(3), 2760–2771. https://doi.org/10.1007/s12144-022-02862-9

Benedetto, L., Macidonio, S., & Ingrassia, M. (2024). Well-being and perfectionism: Assessing the mediational role of self-compassion in emerging adults. *European Journal of Investigation in Health, Psychology and Education, 14*(5), 1383–1395. https://doi.org/10.3390/ejihpe14050091

Bensimon, M. (2020). Perceptions of music therapists regarding their work with children living under continuous war threat: Experiential reframing of trauma through songs. *Nordic Journal of Music Therapy, 29*(4), 300–316. https://doi.org/10.1080/08098131.2019.1703210

Bentley, T. G. K., D'Andrea-Penna, G., Rakic, M., Arce, N., LaFaille, M., Berman, R., Cooley, K., & Sprimont, P. (2023). Breathing practices for stress and anxiety reduction: A systematic review. *Brain Sciences, 13*(12), 1612. https://doi.org/10.3390/brainsci13121612

Beumer, M. (2020). The foundation of anthropology to ritual studies. Journal of Ritual Studies, 34(2), 20-30. https://www.jstor.org/stable/48653331

Blanke, E. S., Schmidt, M. J., Riediger, M., & Brose, A. (2020). Thinking mindfully: How mindfulness relates to rumination and reflection in daily life. *Emotion, 20*(8), 1369–1381. https://doi.org/10.1037/emo0000659

Bluth, K., Campo, R. A., Futch, W. S., & Gaylord, S. A. (2017). Age and gender differences in the associations of self-compassion and emotional well-being in a large adolescent sample. *Journal of Youth and Adolescence, 46*(4), 840–853. https://doi.org/10.1007/s10964-016-0567-2

Bly, R. A. (1989). *Little book on the human shadow*. Harper & Row.

Bonini, L., Rotunno, C., Arcuri, E., & Gallese, V. (2022). Mirror neurons 30 years later: Implications and applications. *Trends in Cognitive Sciences, 26*(9), 767–781. https://doi.org/10.1016/j.tics.2022.06.003

Bowlby, J. (2012). *A secure base*. Taylor & Francis.

Bożek, A., & Nowak, P. F. (2020). The relationship between spirituality, health-related behavior, and psychological well-being. *Frontiers in Psychology, 11*, Article 1997. https://doi.org/10.3389/fpsyg.2020.01997

Brach, T. (2019). *Radical compassion: Learning to love yourself and your world*. Viking.

Brandmayr, F. (2021). Social science as apologia. *European Journal of Social Theory, 24*(3), 319–337. https://doi.org/10.1177/1368431021990965

Brown, D. P., & Elliott, D. S. (2016). *Attachment disturbances in adults: Treatment for comprehensive repair*. W. W. Norton & Co.

Chida, Y., Steptoe, A., & Powell, L. H. (2009). Religiosity/spirituality and mortality: A systematic quantitative review. *Psychotherapy and Psychosomatics, 78*(2), 81–90. https://doi.org/10.1159/000190791

Chowkase, A. A., Parra-Martínez, F. A., Ghahremani, M., Bernstein, Z., Finora, G., & Sternberg, R. J. (2024). Dual-process model of courage. *Frontiers in Psychology, 15*, 1376195. https://doi.org/10.3389/fpsyg.2024.1376195

Church, D., Stapleton, P., Vasudevan, A., & O'Keefe, T. (2022). Clinical EFT as an evidence-based practice for the treatment of psychological and physiological conditions: A systematic review. *Frontiers in Psychology, 13*, 951451. https://doi.org/10.3389/fpsyg.2022.951451

Codina, N., Valenzuela, R., & Pestana, J. V. (2018). Relations between student procrastination and teaching styles: Autonomy-supportive vs. controlling. *Frontiers in Psychology, 9*, Article 809. https://doi.org/10.3389/fpsyg.2018.00809

Corrigan, F. M., Fisher, J. J., & Nutt, D. J. (2010). Autonomic dysregulation and the window of tolerance model of the effects of complex trauma. *Journal of Psychopharmacology, 25*(1), 17–25. https://doi.org/10.1177/0269881109354930

Csikszentmihalyi, M. (1975). *Beyond boredom and anxiety: Experiencing flow in work and play*. Jossey-Bass.

Dames, S. S. (2018). *A study of the interplay between new graduate life experience, context, and the experience of stress in the workplace: Exploring factors towards self-actualizing as a novice nurse* (Unpublished doctoral thesis). University of Calgary.

Dames, S. (2022). *Root strength: A health and care professionals' guide to minimizing stress and maximizing thriving*. Elsevier.

Davis, A. J., Crittenden, B., & Cohen, E. (2021). Effects of social support on performance outputs and perceived difficulty during physical exercise. *Physiology & Behavior, 239*, Article 113490. https://doi.org/10.1016/j.physbeh.2021.113490

Della Longa, L., Sarlo, M., & Farroni, T. (2025). Does affective touch buffer emotional distress? Insights from subjective and physiological indices. *Social Cognitive and Affective Neuroscience, 20*(1), nsaf090. https://doi.org/10.1093/scan/nsaf090

Dennis, A., & Ogden, J. (2025). The role of emotion regulation in body-focused gratitude: Impacts on well-being, body compassion, and behavioural intentions. *International Journal of Applied Positive Psychology*. Advance online publication. https://doi.org/10.1007/s41042-025-00220-6

DeSteno, D., Lim, D., & Dickens, L. (2019). The grateful brain: A neuropsychological model of gratitude and its effects on health and well-being. *Emotion Review, 11*(3), 192–207. https://doi.org/10.1177/1754073918765702

DiFonzo, N., Alongi, A., & Wiele, P. (2020). Apology, restitution, and forgiveness after psychological contract breach. *Journal of Business Ethics, 161*(1), 53–69. https://doi.org/10.1007/s10551-018-3984-1

Durkheim, E. (1912). *The elementary forms of the religious life.* Allen & Unwin.

Ehrhardt, K., & Ensher, E. (2021). Perceiving a calling, living a calling, and calling outcomes: How mentoring matters. *Journal of Counseling Psychology, 68*(2), 168–181. https://doi.org/10.1037/cou0000513

Ehrmann, M. (1927/2023). *Desiderata.* Public-domain poem. (Original work published 1927; entered the public domain in Canada and other jurisdictions in 2023). https://en.wikipedia.org/wiki/Desiderata

Einstein, A. (1972). *Ideas and opinions* (Based on *Mein Weltbild,* edited by Carl Seelig; S. Bargmann, Trans.). Crown Publishers. (Original work published 1949).

Emmons, R. A., Hill, P. C., Barrett, J. L., & Kapic, K. M. (2017). Psychological and theological reflections on grace and its relevance for science and practice. *Psychology of Religion and Spirituality, 9*(3), 276–284. https://doi.org/10.1037/rel0000136

Folmer, C. P., Wildschut, T., Haesevoets, T., De Keersmaecker, J., Van Assche, J., & Van Lange, P. A. M. (2022). Repairing trust between individuals and groups: The effectiveness of apologies in interpersonal and intergroup contexts. *Social Psychological and Personality Science, 13*(4), 791–800. https://doi.org/10.1177/19485506211024073

Foster, A., Van Tongeren, D. R., Fritz, J., & Steptoe, A. (2023). Social connection and mortality in UK Biobank: A prospective cohort analysis. *BMC Medicine, 21,* Article 316. https://doi.org/10.1186/s12916-023-03055-7

Fu, Y., Wang, D., Liu, J., Wang, H., Wen, F., Chen, W., & Liu, Z. (2025). The shared neural substrates of emotional mimicry and emotional contagion: An activation likelihood estimation meta-analysis and meta-analytic connectivity modeling analysis. *Social Cognitive and Affective Neuroscience, 20*(1), nsaf091. https://doi.org/10.1093/scan/nsaf091

Garland, E. L., Farb, N. A., Goldin, P. R., & Fredrickson, B. L. (2015). Mindfulness broadens awareness and builds eudaimonic meaning: A process model of mindful positive emotion regulation. *Psychological Inquiry, 26*(4), 293–314. https://doi.org/10.1080/1047840X.2015.1064294

Gilar-Corbi, R., Izquierdo, A., & Castejón, J.-L. (2025). Structural model of emotional intelligence, resilience, and stress in university students. *Behavioral Sciences, 15*(7), 894. https://doi.org/10.3390/bs15070894

Goldberg, S. B., Riordan, K. M., Sun, S., & Davidson, R. J. (2022). The empirical status of mindfulness-based interventions: A systematic review of 44 meta-analyses of randomized controlled trials. *Perspectives on Psychological Science, 17*(1), 108–130. https://doi.org/10.1177/1745691620968771

Gollan, J. K., Hoxha, D., Hunnicutt-Ferguson, K., Norris, C. J., Rosebrock, L., Sankin, L., & Cacioppo, J. (2016). Twice the negativity bias and half the positivity offset: Evaluative responses to emotional information in depression. *Journal of Behavior Therapy and Experimental Psychiatry, 52,* 166–170. https://doi.org/10.1016/j.jbtep.2015.09.005

Grass, A., Rosner, R., Ciner, A., Wiegand-Grefe, S., & Goldbeck, L. (2025). Therapeutic alliance during trauma-focused treatment in adolescent and young adult patients with PTSD. *BMC Psychiatry, 25*(1), 38. https://doi.org/10.1186/s12888-024-06410-x

Greenberg, L. S., & Goldman, R. N. (Eds.). (2019). *Clinical handbook of emotion-focused therapy.* American Psychological Association. https://doi.org/10.1037/0000112-000

Grizzlypaws, L. (2023). Strengthening our resilience through land-based teaching and learning knowledge transmission. *Indigenous Graduate Student Symposium Journal, 3*(1). https://journals.lib.sfu.ca/index.php/igss/article/view/6203

Grof, S. (2013). Revision and re-enchantment of psychology: Legacy from half a century of consciousness research. In H. L. Friedman & G. Hartelius (Eds.), *The Wiley-Blackwell handbook of transpersonal psychology* (pp. 91–120). https://doi.org/10.1002/9781118591277.ch5

Grof, S., & Grof, C. (2010). *Holotropic breathwork: A new approach to self-exploration and therapy.* State University of New York Press.

Gunnell, K. E., Mosewich, A. D., McEwen, C. E., Eklund, R. C., & Crocker, P. R. E. (2017). Don't be so hard on yourself! Changes in self-compassion during the first year of university are associated with changes in well-being. *Personality and Individual Differences, 107,* 43–48. https://doi.org/10.1016/j.paid.2016.11.032

Hāfez. (1999). Don't surrender your loneliness (D. Ladinsky, Trans.). In D. Ladinsky (Trans.), *The gift: Poems by Hafiz, the great Sufi master* (pp. 34–35). Penguin Compass.

Harmon-Jones, E., & Peterson, C. K. (2009). Supine body position reduces neural response to anger evocation. *Psychological Science, 20*(10), 1209–1210. https://doi.org/10.1111/j.1467-9280.2009.02416.x

Hasani, J., Mohammadkhani, P., Rezaei, A. M., & Borjali, A. (2025). Evaluating the efficacy of rumination-focused cognitive-behavioural therapy in alleviating depression, negative affect, and rumination among patients with recurrent major depressive disorder. *BMC Psychiatry, 25*(1), 92. https://doi.org/10.1186/s12888-025-07065-y

Hermans, E. J., Hendler, T., & Kalisch, R. (2025). Building resilience: The stress response as a driving force for neuroplasticity and adaptation. *Biological Psychiatry, 97*(4), 330–338. https://doi.org/10.1016/j.biopsych.2024.10.016

Hobson, N. M., Schroeder, J., Risen, J. L., Xygalatas, D., & Inzlicht, M. (2018). The psychology of rituals: An integrative review and process-based framework. *Personality and Social Psychology Review, 22*(3), 260–284. https://doi.org/10.1177/1088868317734944

Ho, W. W. Y. (2022). Influence of play on positive psychological development in emerging adulthood: A serial mediation model. *Frontiers in Psychology, 13,* Article 1057557. https://doi.org/10.3389/fpsyg.2022.1057557

Homan, K. J., & Sirois, F. M. (2017). Self-compassion and physical health: Exploring the roles of perceived stress and health-promoting behaviours. *Health Psychology Open, 4*(2), 2055102917729542. https://doi.org/10.1177/2055102917729542

Honey, C. J., Mahabal, A., & Bellana, B. (2023). Psychological momentum. *Current Directions in Psychological Science,* 1–9. https://www.honeylab.org

Huang, W., Hall, A. F., Kawalec, N., Opalka, A. N., Liu, J., & Wang, D. V. (2025). Anterior cingulate cortex in complex associative learning: Monitoring action state and action content. *eLife.* https://doi.org/10.7554/eLife.105774.1

Humphrey, C., & Laidlaw, J. (1994). *The Archetypal Actions of Ritual: A Theory of Ritual Illustrated by the Jain Rite of Worship.* Oxford University Press.

Hwang, S., Kim, G., Yang, J., & Yang, E. (2016). The moderating effects of age on the relationships of self-compassion, self-esteem, and mental health: Self-compassion and age. *Japanese Psychological Research, 58*(2), 194–205. https://doi.org/10.1111/jpr.12109

Interfaith Prayers. (n.d.). A Buddhist prayer of forgiveness. Retrieved October 12, 2025, from https://interfaithprayers.com/index.php/2024/08/15/a-buddhist-prayer-of-forgiveness/

Irving, G., Wright, A., & Hibbert, P. (2019). Threshold concept learning: Emotions and liminal space transitions. *Management Learning, 50*(3), 273–290. https://doi.org/10.1177/1350507618822217

Jeserich, F., Klein, C., Brinkhaus, B., & Teut, M. (2023). Sense of coherence and religion/spirituality: A systematic review and meta-analysis based on a methodical classification of instruments measuring religion/spirituality. *PLoS ONE, 18*(8), e0289203. https://doi.org/10.1371/journal.pone.0289203

Joseph, L. (2021). Walking on our lands again: Turning to culturally important plants and Indigenous conceptualizations of health in a time of cultural and political resurgence. *International Journal of Indigenous Health, 16*(1), 165–179. https://doi.org/10.32799/ijih.v16i1.33205

Joseph, L. (2023). *Held by the Land: A Guide to Indigenous Plants for Wellness.* Wellfleet Press.

Jung, C. G. (1959). *Aion: Researches into the phenomenology of the self* (R. F. C. Hull, Trans.; Vol. 9, Part II, pp. 69–70, para. 126). Princeton University Press. (Original work published 1951)

Kabat-Zinn, J. (2003). Mindfulness-based interventions in context: Past, present, and future. *Clinical Psychology: Science and Practice, 10*(2), 144–156. https://doi.org/10.1093/clipsy.bpg016

Kafle, E., Papastavrou Brooks, C., Chawner, D., Foye, U., Declercq, D., & Brooks, H. (2023). "Beyond laughter": A systematic review to understand how interventions utilise comedy for individuals experiencing mental health problems. *Frontiers in Psychology, 14,* Article 1161703. https://doi.org/10.3389/fpsyg.2023.1161703

Kaur, R. (n.d.). We are all born so beautiful. The greatest tragedy is being convinced we are not [Quote]. Retrieved from https://www.instagram.com/rupikaur_

Kelly, A. C., Vimalakanthan, K., & Miller, K. E. (2014). Self-compassion moderates the relationship between body mass index and both eating disorder pathology and body image flexibility. *Body Image, 11*(4), 446–453. https://doi.org/10.1016/j.bodyim.2014.07.005

Kelly, J. (2018). Forgiveness: A key resiliency builder. *Clinical Orthopaedics and Related Research, 476*(2), 203–204. https://doi.org/10.1007/s11999.0000000000000024

Kidd, T., Devine, S. L., & Walker, S. C. (2023). Affective touch and regulation of stress responses. *Health Psychology Review, 17*(1), 60–77. https://doi.org/10.1080/17437199.2022.2143854

Koenig, H. G. (2012). *Religion, spirituality, and health: The research and clinical implications.* ISRN Psychiatry, 2012, 278730. https://doi.org/10.5402/2012/278730

Ladinsky, D. (1999). *The gift: Poems by Hafiz, the great Sufi master.* Penguin Compass.

Ladinsky, D. (2002). *Love poems from God: Twelve sacred voices from the East and West.* Penguin Compass.

Lally, P., van Jaarsveld, C. H. M., Potts, H. W. W., & Wardle, J. (2010). How are habits formed: Modelling habit formation in the real world. *European Journal of Social Psychology, 40*(6), 998–1009. https://doi.org/10.1002/ejsp.674

Lazare, A. (2004). *On apology.* Oxford University Press.

Lee, L. O., Grodstein, F., Trudel-Fitzgerald, C., James, P., Okuzono, S. S., Koga, H. K., Schwartz, J., Spiro, A., Mroczek, D. K., & Kubzansky, L. D. (2022). Optimism, daily stressors, and emotional well-being over two decades in a cohort of aging men. *The Journals of Gerontology: Series B, Psychological Sciences and Social Sciences, 77*(8), 1373–1383. https://doi.org/10.1093/geronb/gbac025

Lee, L., James, P., Zevon, E., Kim, E., Trudel-Fitzgerald, C., Spiro, A., Grodstein, F., & Kubzansky, L. (2019). Optimism is associated with exceptional longevity in 2 epidemiologic cohorts of men and women. *Proceedings of the National Academy of Sciences.* https://doi.org/10.1073/pnas.1900712116

Lee, J. C., Greenaway, J. K., Don, H. J., & Livesey, E. J. (2024). What makes a stimulus worthy of attention: Cue–outcome correlation and choice relevance in the learned predictiveness effect. *Journal of Experimental Psychology: Learning, Memory, and Cognition, 50*(12), 1875–1891. https://doi.org/10.1037/xlm0001365

Lei, A. A., Phang, V. W. X., Lee, Y. Z., Kow, A. S. F., Tham, C. L., Ho, Y.-C., & Lee, M. T. (2025). Chronic stress-associated depressive disorders: The impact of HPA axis dysregulation and neuroinflammation on the hippocampus—A mini review. *International Journal of Molecular Sciences, 26*(7), 2940. https://doi.org/10.3390/ijms26072940

León-Pérez, G., Martín-Albo, J., Notario-Pacheco, B., Gallego-Beuter, J. L., & Pérez-Yus, M. C. (2012). Spanish adaptation of the perceived stress scale (PSS-14): Psychometric properties. *Psicothema, 24*(2), 305–311.

Lindsay, E. K., Young, S., Brown, K. W., Smyth, J. M., & Creswell, J. D. (2019). Mindfulness training reduces loneliness and increases social contact in a randomized controlled trial. *Proceedings of the National Academy of Sciences of the United States of America, 116*(9), 3488–3493. https://doi.org/10.1073/pnas.1813588116

Liu, X., Li, J., & Chen, X. (2025). Does compassion for oneself extend to prosocial behaviour for others? Examining the relationship between self-compassion and prosocial behaviour using multilevel meta-analysis. *Personality and Individual Differences, 220,* 113047. https://doi.org/10.1016/j.paid.2025.113047

London, M., Sessa, V. I., & Shelley, L. A. (2023). Developing self-awareness: Learning processes for self- and interpersonal growth. *Annual Review of Organizational Psychology and Organizational Behavior, 10*(1), 261–288.

Long, K. N. G., Symons, X., VanderWeele, T. J., Balboni, T. A., Rosmarin, D. H., Puchalski, C., Cutts, T., Gunderson, G. R., Idler, E., Oman, D., Balboni, M. J., Tuach, L. S., & Koh, H. K. (2024). Spirituality as a determinant of health: Emerging policies, practices, and systems. *Health Affairs, 43*(6), 783–790. https://doi.org/10.1377/hlthaff.2023.01643

Luo, Q., Li, X., Zhao, J., Jiang, Q., & Wei, D. (2025). The effect of slow breathing in regulating anxiety. *Scientific Reports, 15,* Article 8417. https://doi.org/10.1038/s41598-025-8417

Ly, C., Greb, A. C., Cameron, L. P., Wong, J. M., Barragan, E. V., Wilson, P. C., ... & Olson, D. E. (2018). Psychedelics promote structural and functional neural plasticity. *Cell Reports, 23*(11), 3170–3182. https://doi.org/10.1016/j.celrep.2018.05.022

Lynch, J. M., Stange, K. C., Dowrick, C., Getz, L., Meredith, P. J., Van Driel, M. L., Harris, M. G., Tillack, K., & Tapp, C. (2025). The sense of safety theoretical framework: A trauma-informed and healing-oriented approach for whole person care. *Frontiers in Psychology, 15,* Article 1441493. https://doi.org/10.3389/fpsyg.2024.1441493

Macfarlane, C., Masthoff, E., & Hakvoort, L. (2019). Short-term music therapy attention and arousal regulation treatment (SMAART) for prisoners with posttraumatic stress disorder: A feasibility study. *Journal of Forensic Psychology Research and Practice, 19*(5), 376–392. https://doi.org/10.1080/24732850.2019.1670023

Maslow, A. H. (1943). A theory of human motivation. *Psychological Review, 50*(4), 370–396. https://doi.org/10.1037/h0054346

McCraty, R. (2016). *Science of the heart, volume 2: Exploring the role of the heart in human performance—An overview of research conducted by the HeartMath Institute.* HeartMath Institute. https://doi.org/10.13140/RG.2.1.3873.5128

McDonald, M. (2021). *Meditation: A practice of* RAIN [Audio talk]. Dharma Seed. https://dharmaseed.org/talks/67471/

McEwen, B. S. (1998). Protective and damaging effects of stress mediators. *New England Journal of Medicine, 338*(3), 171–179. https://doi.org/10.1056/NEJM199801153380307

Mikulincer, M., & Shaver, P. R. (2016). *Attachment in adulthood: Structure, dynamics, and change* (2nd ed.). The Guilford Press.

Mittelmark, M. B. (2021). Resilience in the salutogenic model of health. In M. Ungar (Ed.), *Multisystemic resilience: Adaptation and transformation in contexts of change* (pp. 153–164). Oxford University Press.

Mróz, J., & Kaleta, K. (2023). Forgive, let go, and stay well! The relationship between forgiveness and physical and mental health in women and men: The mediating role of self-consciousness. *International Journal of Environmental Research and Public Health, 20*(13), 6229. https://doi.org/10.3390/ijerph20136229

Neff, K. D. (2003). Self-compassion: An alternative conceptualization of a healthy attitude toward oneself. *Self and Identity, 2*(2), 85–101. https://doi.org/10.1080/15298860309032

Neff, K., & Germer, C. (2018). *The mindful self-compassion workbook: A proven way to accept yourself, build inner strength, and thrive.* The Guilford Press.

Neff, K. (2018). *Self-compassion. Centre for Mindful Self-Compassion.* http://self-compassion.org/the-three-elements-of-self-compassion-2/

Nepo, M. (2004). *The book of awakening: Having the life you want by being present to the life you have.* Conari Press.

Nguyen-Feng, V. N., Ramirez, M., Behrens, K. L., Usset, T., Claussen, A. M., Parikh, R. R., Lee, E. K., Mendenhall, T., Wilt, T. J., & Butler, M. (2025). Trauma-informed care: A systematic review (AHRQ Publication No. 25-EHC007). Agency for Healthcare Research and Quality.

Niebuhr, R. (c. 1932–1933). The serenity prayer [Unpublished prayer]. In R. M. Brown (Ed.), *The essential Reinhold Niebuhr: Selected essays and addresses* (pp. 251–252). Yale University Press, 1986.

Nummenmaa, L., Hari, R., Hietanen, J. K., & Glerean, E. (2018). Maps of subjective feelings. *Proceedings of the National Academy of Sciences of the United States of America, 115*(37), 9198–9203. https://doi.org/10.1073/pnas.1807390115

162

O'Connor, M., Stapleton, A., O'Reilly, G., Murphy, E., Connaughton, L., Hoctor, E., & McHugh, L. (2023). The efficacy of mindfulness-based interventions in promoting resilience: A systematic review and meta-analysis of randomized controlled trials. *Journal of Contextual Behavioral Science, 28*, 215–225. https://doi.org/10.1016/j.jcbs.2023.03.005

O'Donohue, J. (2002). *Benedictus: A book of blessings.* Bantam.

Ogden, P., & Fisher, J. (2015). *Sensorimotor psychotherapy: Interventions for trauma and attachment.* W. W. Norton & Company.

Olivetti, K. (2023). Kintsugi—Art of repair: An interview with Morty Bachar. *Jung Journal, 17*(3), 131–141. https://doi.org/10.1080/19342039.2023.2224729

Orbell, S., & Verplanken, B. (2020). Changing behavior using habit theory. In M. S. Hagger, L. D. Cameron, K. Hamilton, N. Hankonen, & T. Lintunen (Eds.), *The handbook of behavior change* (pp. 178–192). Cambridge University Press. https://doi.org/10.1017/9781108677318.013

Oschman, J. L. (2000). *Energy medicine: The scientific basis.* Churchill Livingstone.

Panksepp, J., & Biven, L. (2012). *The archaeology of mind: Neuroevolutionary origins of human emotions.* W. W. Norton & Company

Park, J., Bluth, K., Lathren, C., Leary, M., & Hoyle, R. (2024). The synergy between stress and self-compassion in building resilience: A 4-year longitudinal study. *Social and Personality Psychology Compass, 18*(7), Article e12978. https://doi.org/10.1111/spc3.12978

Porges, S. W. (2011). *The polyvagal theory: Neurophysiological foundations of emotions, attachment, communication, and self-regulation.* W. W. Norton.

Porges, S. W. (2022). Polyvagal theory: A science of safety. *Frontiers in Integrative Neuroscience, 16*, 871227. https://doi.org/10.3389/fnint.2022.871227

Proyer, R. T. (2014). To love and play: Testing the association of adult playfulness with the relationship personality and relationship satisfaction. *Current Psychology, 33*(4), 501–514. https://doi.org/10.1007/s12144-014-9225-6

Pury, C. L. S., Starkey, C. B., & Olson, L. R. (2024). Value of goal predicts accolade courage: More evidence that courage is taking a worthwhile risk. *The Journal of Positive Psychology, 19*(2), 236–242. https://doi.org/10.1080/17439760.2023.2178959

Querdasi, F. R., & Callaghan, B. L. (2023). A translational approach to the mind–brain–body connection [Editorial]. *Translational Issues in Psychological Science, 9*(2), 103–106. https://doi.org/10.1037/tps0000374

Ram Dass, & Gorman, P. (1985). *How can I help? Stories and reflections on service.* Alfred A. Knopf.

Ray, D. C. (2019). *Play therapy* (ACA Practice Briefs). American Counseling Association

Rogers, C. (1959). A theory of therapy, personality and interpersonal relationships as developed in the client-centered framework. In S. Koch (Ed.), *Psychology: A study of a science. Vol. 3: Formulations of the person and the social context* (pp. 184–256). McGraw Hill.

Rohr, R. (1999). *Everything belongs: The gift of contemplative prayer.* The Crossroad Publishing Company.

Rosenberg, M. B. (2015). *Nonviolent communication: A language of life* (3rd ed.). Puddle Dancer Press.

Rowland, L., & Curry, O. S. (2019). A range of kindness activities boost happiness. *The Journal of Social Psychology, 159*(3), 340–343. https://doi.org/10.1080/00224545.2018.1469461

Russo-Netzer, P., & Atad, O. I. (2024). Activating values intervention: An integrative pathway to well-being. *Frontiers in Psychology, 15*, 1375237. https://doi.org/10.3389/fpsyg.2024.1375237

Sá, R. (2025). Human biofield components explained: A tensegrity-based biophysical framework for energy medicine. *International Journal of Complementary and Alternative Medicine, 18*(2).

Sabo Mordechay, D., Nir, B., & Eviatar, Z. (2019). Expressive writing—Who is it good for? Individual differences in the improvement of mental health resulting from expressive writing. *Complementary Therapies in Clinical Practice, 37*, 115–121. https://doi.org/10.1016/j.ctcp.2019.101064

Sahdra, B. K., Shaver, P. R., & Brown, K. W. (2010). A scale to measure nonattachment: A Buddhist complement to Western research on attachment and adaptive functioning. Journal of Personality Assessment, 92(2), 116–127. https://doi.org/10.1080/00223890903425960

Savage, B. M., Lujan, H. L., Thipparthi, R. R., & DiCarlo, S. E. (2017). Humor, laughter, learning, and health! A brief review. *Advances in Physiology Education, 41*(3), 341–347. https://doi.org/10.1152/advan.00008.2017

Seok, J., & Kim, J. U. (2024). The effectiveness of emotional freedom techniques for depressive symptoms: A meta-analysis. *Journal of Clinical Medicine, 13*(21), 6481. https://doi.org/10.3390/jcm13216481

Siegel, D. (1999). *The developing mind: Toward a neurobiology of interpersonal experience.* Guilford Press.

Sloshower, J., Zeifman, R. J., Guss, J., Krause, R., Safi-Aghdam, H., Pathania, S., Pittman, B., & D'Souza, D. C. (2024). Psychological flexibility as a mechanism of change in psilocybin-assisted therapy for major depression: Results from an exploratory placebo-controlled trial. *Scientific Reports, 14*, 8833. https://doi.org/10.1038/s41598-024-58318-x

Smith, S. M., & Vela, E. (2001). Environmental context-dependent memory: A review and meta-analysis. *Psychonomic Bulletin & Review, 8*(2), 203–220. https://doi.org/10.3758/BF03196157

Smith, M. A., Thompson, A., Hall, L. J., Allen, S. F., & Wetherell, M. A. (2018). The physical and psychological health benefits of positive emotional writing: Investigating the moderating role of Type D (distressed) personality. *British Journal of Health Psychology, 23*(4), 857–871. https://doi.org/10.1111/bjhp.12320

Solberg Nes, L. S., & Segerstrom, S. C. (2006). Dispositional optimism and coping: A meta-analytic review. *Personality and Social Psychology Review, 10*, 235–251. https://doi.org/10.1207/s15327957pspr1003_3

Somé, S. (2004). *Women's wisdom from the heart of Africa. Sounds True.*

Sujato, B. (Trans.). (2017). Therīgāthā [Verses of the Elder Nuns]. SuttaCentral. https://suttacentral.net/thig/en/sujato

Surzykiewicz, J., Skalski, S. B., Sołbut, A., Rutkowski, S., & Konaszewski, K. (2022). Resilience and regulation of emotions in adolescents: Serial mediation analysis through self-esteem and the perceived social support. *International Journal of Environmental Research and Public Health, 19*(13), 8007. https://doi.org/10.3390/ijerph19138007

Tambiah, S. J. (1979). A performative approach to ritual. *In Proceedings of the British Academy* (Vol. 65, pp. 113–169). Oxford University Press.

Taylor, J. B. (2008). *My stroke of insight: A brain scientist's personal journey* (1st ed.). Viking.

Tonarelli, A., Cosentino, C., Tomasoni, C., Nelli, L., Damiani, I., Goisis, S., Sarli, L., & Artioli, G. (2018). Expressive writing: A tool to help health workers of palliative care. *Acta Bio-Medica: Atenei Parmensis, 89*(6-S), 35–42.

Touroutoglou, A., Andreano, J., Dickerson, B. C., & Barrett, L. F. (2020). The tenacious brain: How the anterior mid-cingulate contributes to achieving goals. *Cortex, 123,* 12–29. https://doi.org/10.1016/j.cortex.2019.09.001

Tremblay, L., Van Gordon, W., & Elander, J. (2024). Toward greater clarity in defining and understanding nonattachment. *Mindfulness, 15*(6), 1275–1288. https://doi.org/10.1007/s12671-024-02378-7

Troy, A. S. (2015). Reappraisal and resilience to stress: Context must be considered. *Behavioral and Brain Sciences, 38,* e123. https://doi.org/10.1017/S0140525X1400171X

Turner, E. (2012). *Communitas: The Anthropology of Collective Joy.* Palgrave MacMillan

Turner, T. (2017). *Belonging: Remembering ourselves home.* Her Own Room Press.

Uvnäs-Moberg, K., & Petersson, M. (2022). Physiological effects induced by stimulation of cutaneous sensory nerves, with a focus on oxytocin. *Current Opinion in Behavioral Sciences, 43,* 159–166. https://doi.org/10.1016/j.cobeha.2021.10.001

Van Der Gaag, M. A. E., Gmelin, O. J. H., & De Ruiter, N. M. P. (2025). Understanding identity development in context: Comparing reflective and situated approaches to identity. *Frontiers in Psychology, 15,* Article 1467280. https://doi.org/10.3389/fpsyg.2024.1467280

Van der Kolk, B. A. (2014). *The body keeps the score: Brain, mind, and body in the healing of trauma.* Viking.

Van Ede, F., Lange, F. P., & Spaak, E. (2025). Rhythmic sampling of attention: Linking perception to action in the human brain. *Journal of Neuroscience, 45*(7), e1616242024. https://doi.org/10.1523/JNEUROSCI.1616-24.2024

VanderWeele, T. J. (2017). Religion and health: A synthesis. In M. J. Balboni & J. R. Peteet (Eds.), *Spirituality and religion within the culture of medicine: From evidence to practice* (pp. 357–401). Oxford University Press.

Waldegrave, C. (1990). Just therapy. *Dulwich Centre Newsletter, 1*(6), 46.

Wallace, D. F. (2009). *This is water: Some thoughts, delivered on a significant occasion, about living a compassionate life.* Little, Brown and Company.

Wang, S., Okada, T., & Takagi, K. (2023). How to effectively overcome fixation: A systematic review of fixation and defixation studies on the basis of fixation source and problem type. *Frontiers in Education, 8,* 1183025. https://doi.org/10.3389/feduc.2023.1183025

Watkins, P. C., Emmons, R. A., Greaves, M. R., & Bell, J. (2018). Joy is a distinct positive emotion: Assessment of joy and relationship to gratitude and well-being. *The Journal of Positive Psychology, 13*(5), 522–539. https://doi.org/10.1080/17439760.2017.1414298

Watts, R., & Luoma, J. B. (2020). The use of the psychological flexibility model to support psychedelic-assisted therapy. *Journal of Contextual Behavioral Science, 15,* 92–102. https://doi.org/10.1016/j.jcbs.2019.12.004

Wei, M., Russell, D. W., Mallinckrodt, B., & Vogel, D. L. (2007). The Experiences in Close Relationship Scale (ECR)-Short Form: Reliability, validity, and factor structure. *Journal of Personality Assessment, 88,* 187–204. https://doi.org/10.1080/00223890701268041

Weingarten, K. (2003). Compassionate witnessing and the transformation of societal violence: How individuals can make a difference. *Human Dignity and Humiliation Studies.*

Whitehead, R., Bates, G., Elphinstone, B., Yang, Y., & Murray, G. (2018). Letting go of self: The creation of the Nonattachment to Self Scale. *Frontiers in Psychology, 9,* Article 2544. https://doi.org/10.3389/fpsyg.2018.02544

Whyte, D. (2015). *Consolations: The solace, nourishment and underlying meaning of everyday words.* Many Rivers Press.

Winter, A. L., & Granqvist, P. (2023). Where the spirit meets the bone: Embodied religiospiritual cognition from an attachment viewpoint. *Religions, 14*(4), 511. https://doi.org/10.3390/rel14040511

Wong, M. Y. C., Fung, H. W., Wong, J. Y., & Lam, S. K. K. (2025). Exploring the longitudinal dynamics of self-criticism, self-compassion, psychological flexibility, and mental health in a three-wave study. *Scientific Reports, 15*(1), 13878. https://doi.org/10.1038/s41598-025-95821-1

Wood, A. M., Joseph, S., Lloyd, J., & Atkins, S. (2009). Gratitude influences sleep through the mechanism of pre-sleep cognitions. *Journal of Psychosomatic Research, 66*(1), 43–48. https://doi.org/10.1016/j.jpsychores.2008.09.002

Wood, A. M., & Maltby, J. J. (2009). Gratitude predicts psychological well-being above the Big Five facets. *Personality and Individual Differences, 46*(4), 443–447. https://doi.org/10.1016/j.paid.2008.11.012

Wyles, P., O'Leary, P., & Tsantefski, M. (2023). Bearing witness as a process for responding to trauma survivors: A review. *Trauma, Violence & Abuse, 24*(5), 3078–3093. https://doi.org/10.1177/15248380221124262

Zhang, X., Wang, M., & Wang, H. (2024). Time perspectives, basic psychological need satisfaction, and procrastination: A moderated mediation model. *BMC Psychology, 12,* 149. https://doi.org/10.1186/s40359-023-01494-8

Zhu, N., Li, C., Ye, Y., Zhang, L., & Kong, F. (2024). Longitudinal effect of gratitude on prosocial behavior among young adults: Evidence from the bi-factor model of gratitude. *Journal of Happiness Studies, 25*(1–2), Article 3. https://doi.org/10.1007/s10902-024-00731-0